# A Message for the Ages

# A Message for the Ages

Joel S. Goldsmith

Edited by
Lorraine Sinkler

Acropolis Books, Publisher
Atlanta, Georgia

Published by Acropolis Books
All rights reserved
Printed in the United States of America

For information contact:
ACROPOLIS BOOKS, INC.
Atlanta, Georgia

www.acropolisbooks.com

---

Library of Congress Cataloging-in-Publication Data

Goldsmith, Joel S., 1892-1964.
  A message for the ages / Joel S. Goldsmith ; edited by Lorraine
Sinkler.
      p. cm.
  ISBN 1-889051-64-0 (pbk.)
  1. Spiritual life. I. Sinkler, Lorraine. II. Title.

BP610.G641595 2003
299'.93--dc21
                                        2003004487

Except the Lord build the house,
they labour in vain that build it. . .

— Psalm 127

⌒

"Illumination dissolves all material ties and binds men together with the golden chains of spiritual understanding; it acknowledges only the leadership of the Christ; it has no ritual or rule but the divine, impersonal universal Love; no other worship than the inner Flame that is ever lit at the shrine of Spirit. This union is the free state of spiritual brotherhood. The only restraint is the discipline of Soul; therefore, we know liberty without license; we are a united universe without physical limits, a divine service to God without ceremony or creed. The illumined walk without fear – by Grace."

— *The Infinite Way* by Joel S. Goldsmith

# Dedication

Twentieth century mystic Joel S. Goldsmith revealed to the Western world the nature and substance of mystical living that demonstrated how mankind can live in the consciousness of God. The clarity and insight of his teachings, called the Infinite Way, were captured in more than thirty-five books and in over twelve hundred hours of tape recordings that, today, perpetuate his message.

Joel faithfully arranged to have prepared from his class tapes, monthly letters which were made available as one of the most important tools to assist students in their study and application of the Infinite Way teachings. He felt each of these letters came from an ever-new insight that would produce a deeper level of understanding and awareness of truth as students worked diligently with this fresh and timely material.

Each yearly compilation of the *Letters* focused on a central theme, and it became apparent that working with an entire year's material built an ascending level of consciousness. The *Letters* were subsequently published as books, each containing all the year's letters. The publications became immensely popular as they proved to be of great assistance in the individual student's development of spiritual awareness.

Starting in 1954, the monthly letters were made availiable to students wishing to subscribe to them. Each year of the *Letters* was published individually during 1954 through 1959 and made available in book form. From 1960 through 1970 the *Letters* were published and renamed as books with the titles:

| | |
|---|---|
| 1960 Letters | *Our Spiritual Resources* |
| 1961 Letters | *The Contemplative Life* |
| 1962 Letters | *Man Was Not Born to Cry* |
| 1963 Letters | *Living Now* |
| 1964 Letters | *Realization of Oneness* |
| 1965 Letters | *Beyond Words and Thoughts* |
| 1966 Letters | *The Mystical I* |
| 1967 Letters | *Living Between Two Worlds* |
| 1968 Letters | *The Altitude of Prayer* |
| 1969 Letters | *Consciousness Is What I Am* |
| 1970 Letters | *Awakening Mystical Consciousness* |

Joel worked closely with his editor, Lorraine Sinkler, to ensure each letter carried the continuity, integrity, and pure consciousness of the message. After Joel's transition in 1964, Emma A. Goldsmith (Joel's wife) requested that Lorraine continue working with the monthly letters, drawing as in the past from the inexhaustible tape recordings of his class work with students. The invaluable work by Lorraine and Emma has ensured that this message will be preserved and available in written form for future generations. Acropolis Books is honored and privileged to offer in book form the next eleven years of Joel's teaching.

The 1971 through 1981 *Letters* also carry a central theme for each year, and have been renamed with the following titles:

| | |
|---|---|
| 1971 Letters | *Living by the Word* |
| 1972 Letters | *Living the Illumined Life* |
| 1973 Letters | *Seek Ye First* |
| 1974 Letters | *Spiritual Discernment: the Healing Consciousness* |
| 1975 Letters | *A Message for the Ages* |
| 1976 Letters | *I Stand on Holy Ground* |
| 1977 Letters | *The Art of Spiritual Living* |
| 1978 Letters | *God Formed Us for His Glory* |
| 1979 Letters | *The Journey Back to the Father's House* |
| 1980 Letters | *Showing Forth the Presence of God* |
| 1981 Letters | *The Only Freedom* |

Acropolis Books dedicates this series of eleven books to Lorraine Sinkler and Emma A. Goldsmith for their ongoing commitment to ensure that these teachings will never be lost to the world.

# Table of Contents

# A Message for the Ages

*Chapter One*

# The Need for Religion

Why do we need religion? The true, full, and complete answer is that we need it for fulfillment; we need it to fulfill ourselves. As human beings we are barren and empty of truth, empty of spiritual light and a knowledge of our source. We are living like a branch of a tree that is cut off, and until we become at-one with the trunk of the tree and with its root and all that is in the ground, the air, and the sky, we are going to remain barren. Through religion—and I do not mean religion in the sense of organized church worship, but religion in the sense of a knowledge of God or the experience of God—we become reunited with our source, fulfilled, and find ourselves reestablished in the Father's house.

We need religion to reunite us with our source in order that we may be fulfilled from within of the Spirit, with the glory of God which no human being can have, for the creature is not under "the law of God, neither indeed can be."[1]

> His grace is upon me; His spirit is upon me; His life
> is my life. I have no life separate and apart from God.
> In heaven or in hell I find that Life, and even if I

"walk through the valley of the shadow of death,"[2]
I still find that God is my life because I have become
consciously at-one with my source.

The life of the tree is the life of the branch, and not
just the life of a branch separate and apart. The life of
the roots is the life of the branch. The life of the soil,
the air, the sun, the moon, the snow, the rain,
the dew—all of this is now the life of the tree.

To a great extent much organized religion has perverted this
teaching and placed its emphasis on praying to God for things
instead of being spiritually fulfilled and letting the things be
added. Its major attention has been given to obeying man-made
rules and laws, observing rites, ceremonies, and creeds, and in a
measure it has overlooked the real purpose of religion which is
not to build churches and have people obey certain creeds but
to guide each person into wholeness and fulfillment through the
spirit of God.

## The Nature of the Spiritual Path Is Fulfillment

As long as man is looked upon merely as a mental and physical being, he is neither fulfilled nor complete. Man is more
than mind and body, and he is complete only when he has realized the nature of his Selfhood, has submitted his mind and
body to his soul, thereby letting the soul govern his thoughts
and bodily action.

It is through truth teachings, especially those embracing
mysticism, that we begin to perceive that God is not to be used
for a personal material purpose or as a servant to man. In mystical truth we learn that we are servants of God, inlets to, and
outlets for, the grace of God. So it is that it will take the mystical teachings to lead the church back to the Father-conscious-

ness and to inspire the metaphysical movements to give up *using* truth, which is a synonym for God, to demonstrate shoes, automobiles, houses, marriages, and divorces.

The nature of the spiritual path is fulfillment. We must stop thinking of it in terms of health, wealth, happiness, peace of mind, or even peace on earth. How can there be peace on earth unless we are fulfilled spiritually? How can there be peace even in a little group of students on the mystical path unless there is spiritual fulfillment? If they are not fulfilled spiritually one or more of them is going to begin to get human—physically, mentally, morally, or financially. Only in proportion to our spiritual fulfillment can we act like children of God, and when that happens there will be no more envy, lust, or greed. Love will take on a different nature. It will be built not on my rights and your rights, but on our spiritual fulfillment and the sharing of that.

### *The Old Concept of God Does Not Satisfy Modern Man*

In today's age of scientific enlightenment, the God the world has prayed to ever since the days of Abraham, Isaac, and Jacob does not satisfy people. They are now saying, "Prove it to us. You have told us that we have to be baptized in order to be in God's grace, but those of us who are baptized are no better off than our unbaptized neighbors. You have told us we must go to communion or to confession, but we are no better off after that than our neighbor next door. When there is unemployment we are unemployed and our neighbor is unemployed, and when there is an epidemic we all get sick." It may be that these ideas are not formulated in words, but that is what many people are thinking.

With the advent of Christian Science, Unity, and New Thought, people began to switch their concepts of God from one with whom they begged and pleaded to one they could use, but they perpetuated the idea that the new God they had found would do for them the things that the old God had not done. The old God did not provide them with automobiles, and the old God did not heal their diseases, but now the new God will.

## *Only One God*

There is only one God. Whether we are dealing with black or white, Jew or Gentile, there is only one God. This acknowledgment will break down racial prejudice and bias. As long as people believe there is a Hebrew God, a Protestant God, a Catholic God, or a Vedantist God, there will be bigotry.

The world must stop believing that Krishna is God, that Buddha is God, or that Jesus is God, and begin to realize that God is God. East and West, North and South, white and black, Jew and Christian, God alone is God, and that God has no religion and no personality. That God in Its infinity is manifest in the individuality of man, so whether a person is a Jew, a Christian, a Buddhist, or an atheist, he is the same God-man, regardless of what he thinks himself to be, for God existed "before Abraham was,"[3] and God will exist to the end of the world. With or without religion, God is. God manifests as the life, mind, and soul of individual being, and in this recognition of the impersonal nature of God, fear must disappear. God is the God of the just and of the unjust; God is no respecter of persons; God is the God of the saint and of the sinner. There is no absence of the universal impersonal God.

## *Spiritual Enlightenment Rejects*
## *the God of Hell-Fire and Damnation*

The God we worship is the same God everyone else worships, albeit in different forms of worship. But God is the one and the same God, because there cannot be more than one. There is only one Father, and He is your Father and my Father.

Whether I go to church or do not go to church, He is still my Father, and God cannot any more cast me off than He cast off the Prodigal Son. The Prodigal Son can take himself away from the Father, but in any minute that he turns back, the Father is there waiting for him. The Father did not excommunicate the Prodigal. The Father did not excommunicate the woman taken in adultery; the Father did not excommunicate the thief on the cross. In the instant they turned to Him, there was the Father, there was the Christ.

### Wrong-Doing Sets Up a Reaction Within Ourselves

At the center of your being and mine there is a rightness which we can call our conscience or the God that sees in secret. However the idea is expressed, at the center of our being there is a sense of rightness. When we do wrong and violate our highest sense of right, that wrong hits up against our center of rightness, and from that minute on a friction and turmoil are set up in us which may appear outwardly as problems of one kind or another. We are apparently being punished, but we are not being punished by God.

God constitutes our being. God has breathed His life into us, not our life, His life. The mind or intelligence of God is ours; we do not have any intelligence separate and apart from God. As a matter of fact, we do not have a soul of our own: God is the very soul of our being. Our whole being is God-being, God-essence, and anything that is brought into the orbit of that being that is not right sets up a warfare between the spirit and the flesh. That reaction is not from God to us, any more than electricity is aware of giving us a shock or electrocuting us if it is hooked up incorrectly.

Just as the Orientals have embraced the law of karma as a basic part of their teaching, so we in Christianity have accepted the same law in the doctrine of as-ye-sow-so-shall-ye-reap, which means that every minute of the day and night we are setting in motion the law that will ultimately react upon us. The more closely we live according to spiritual standards, the more sensitive we are to the spirit and the less wrong we can do without injury to ourselves. The least kind of skulduggery will react upon the individual who violates his own spiritual integrity.

On the other hand, the person who is gross, who has never lived very close to God or thought much about God can go on for a long time storing up karma. When it reaches a certain level, however, even he gets clipped, because he is not violating *a* God, he is violating *his* God, the God at the center of his being.

### An Inner Cleansing Is Necessary for Forgiveness

When we take the Master's teaching seriously, we realize that we cannot merely go to church on Sunday and because of that receive absolution. No minister, priest, or rabbi can absolve us while we remain in the same old consciousness. This the Master illustrated when he said to the woman taken in adultery: "Neither do I condemn thee: go, and sin no more."[4] In other words, absolution lasts for today. It can be permanent only if we are willing to make it so, but if we sin tomorrow a worse thing will come upon us.

If we are full of sorrow and regret for what we may have done, in that proportion we are made free by the very spirit of God that is in us, but it is imperative that we go and sin no more. This involves a quite different concept of God than we may have had before. Heretofore as long as we had some prayers said over us, we were forgiven and we felt holy, but now an inner cleansing is demanded of us. The Master's ministry was always addressed to what individuals must do to fit themselves to receive God's grace.

All of us must ask ourselves the question: What kind of a God do I have? As long as we have a God that can be made to break His own laws, we do not have God. No one, not even God, can do anything for us except in proportion to our willingness to conform to the laws of God.

### *What Is the Righteousness Beyond That of the Scribes and Pharisees?*

Obedience to the Ten Commandments is a long way from obedience to God. The Ten Commandments are merely the laws of human beings. It is like obeying a legal law which a person could obey and still not be spiritual. The Master brought that out when he said, "Except your righteousness shall exceed the righteousness of the scribes and Pharisees, ye shall in no case enter into the kingdom of heaven."[5] Who could exceed the righteousness of the scribes and Pharisees? They obeyed the Ten Commandments; they lived up to every letter of the law; they crossed their t's and dotted their i's. How could a person be holier than that? But the Master was making it clear to his disciples that there is a holiness greater than that of merely obeying the laws of the Ten Commandments which are the laws for human beings.

Until we have a God of spirit, a God of omnipresence, a God of omnipotence, and a God of omniscience, we cannot possibly know what spiritual laws are. There is a righteousness that exceeds that of the scribes and the Pharisees: loving our neighbor, praying for our enemy, considering our neighbor's children as well as our own children, which is not what we call human love, but the divine love that looks upon all as neighbors or brothers. When we see that there is only one God, that God is the creator of all, and that God is the God of our neighbor, even of our atheist neighbor, as well as the God of ourselves, we are living in God's grace. We are a brother to all men, and in this way we begin to have a higher concept of God. Paul speaks of "a man in Christ."[6] That man is the man who has the spirit of God indwelling.

To have the spirit of God indwelling brings God right down to where we can realize:

> The place whereon thou standest is holy ground.
>                                           Exodus 3:5

> Whither shall I go from thy spirit? or whither
>      shall I flee from thy presence?
> If I ascend up into heaven, thou art there:
> if I make my bed in hell, behold, thou art there.
>      If I take the wings of the morning,
>   and dwell in the uttermost parts of the sea;
>      Even there shall thy hand lead me,
>      and thy right hand shall hold me.
>                                      Psalm 139:7-10

> For I am persuaded, that neither death,
> nor life, nor angels, nor principalities, nor powers,
>    nor things present, nor things to come,
>         Nor height, nor depth,
>         nor any other creature,
> shall be able to separate me from the love of God.
>                                      Romans 8:38,39

### *No Withholding God*

God neither gives nor withholds. If there were a God that gave, it must be because He was withholding. But what could God withhold? The diamonds that are in the ground, the oil, the silver, the gold, the platinum, the uranium, the fish in the sea, the birds in the air, the salt in the ocean, the crops in the ground, the cattle on a thousand hills? What is God withholding? Nothing! Is God saying, "I will let it loose when you do something"? No! We could look this whole world over and not find one thing that God is withholding.

True, there is no God that backs things up to our doorway and there is no God that puts oil companies' names on oil, or the diamond syndicate's name on diamonds. That is the work of man. But there is a God, a God that has sent forth this universe into expression, filled with everything we will ever need.

I came across an old edition of the *Encyclopedia Britannica* that referred to uranium as a worthless metal found in North America. It may have been worthless then, but evidently even when it seemed to be worthless it had been provided for atomic use, but certainly not for use in the making of bombs. That is man's idea. There is an Intelligence, and just as God is love, so God is intelligence, the intelligence of nature, and the intelligence of mankind.

One day I watched three myna birds out on the lawn after a day's supply of bread and seeds had been thrown out, enough to satisfy perhaps forty or fifty birds. Two of the birds found pieces of bread, and the third bird was chasing the other two, trying to get their pieces of bread. Right in back of the third bird was a yard full of bread, but he would not give them peace. He must have their particular pieces of bread. We are like that, too. We are determined to have things the way we think they should be, when right next to us is more than we can use if only we could open our eyes to see it.

### *God Is the Soul of Man and the Universe*

If we know that God is the soul of mankind and recognize God as the soul of every individual, that is what comes back to us. If we recognize God to be the intelligence of this universe, we are not only governed intelligently, but those who come into our experience are also governed intelligently in their relationship with us.

If we recognize God to be the love of this universe, we cannot know lack, because we are not looking to man for supply. It will come through man, but what a mess we would be in if we looked *to* man for it. How man wants to hold onto his dollars! He does not object to parting with them for a color TV, and a woman does not object to using her dollars for a new hairdo, but the church or a spiritual ministry, that is measured in different terms! If we expect man to support a spiritual ministry, we will be hitting up against selfishness and man's fear for his own supply.

If we can understand that God is the love of this universe, then God is the source of our supply. It may still come to us through man, although it does not have to because there are many other ways for it to come. The point is that in looking to God we will never be limited. But we cannot have a God that we fear might be withholding because we have a wrong thought; we cannot have a God that is punishing us because of our parents' or our grandparents' sins.

Our only hope of living under the intelligence, love, and wisdom of God and in fellowship with man is in our ability to see that God is the very soul of man, the very intelligence, and the very love of man.

This is true with all nature. Weather is not a phenomenon of nature. Weather is a phenomenon of the mind of man, and experiments have proved that it can be changed when it becomes rambunctious and destructive. We have proved that the person who lives in the realization of God as the soul of nature will have better crops, whether in his garden or on his farm, or a more productive herd, because he is not looking to the ground for food exclusively. He is standing on a principle revealed by the Master: "Man shall not live by bread alone, but by every word that proceedeth out of the mouth of God."[7]

If God is the soul of this universe, It must be the principle of the animal world as well as of the human. God could not have made man and left the animals out in the cold, could He? That all is a part of God's creation, and God must be the animating principle of all nature. God must be the basic law behind it, or where does this law of nature come from? God must permeate the entire universe, and as we see and understand this, then whatever destructive forces there are disappear.

### Consciousness Is the Secret of Life

This brings us back to the subject of what God is. In revelations or unfoldments that have come to me over a period of time, the word *consciousness* for me became the word God. Suppose we had no consciousness, would we be conscious? Could we be conscious of anything without consciousness? In other words, what is it that makes us aware of one another? What is it that makes us aware of laws of God or laws of nature? Do we not have to become conscious of those things, or in the Master's language, "know the truth"[8]? How can we *know* the truth? Does not *knowing* mean conscious of or aware of? The secret of all life is consciousness. Consciousness permeates everything there is.

When I am meditating or teaching or doing my mail, the birds are singing and often trying to get into the room where I am sitting. Do you think they do not know what is attracting them? When there are animals around, they will come right to the doorway and sit there until we have finished our meditation, and then they leave. Within a very short time cats and dogs stop chasing birds. They are no longer on the prowl. Why? The one Consciousness permeates this entire universe, and that consciousness is God. As we recognize It, everything and everybody become aware of It.

### What Is the Will of God?

There cannot be a God that would injure, destroy, or withhold. Such a God would not be God. God is love, and what makes us believe in Christianity is the life the Master lived and the work he did. He said that his work was "to do the will of him that sent"[9] him. In that will there is no withholding, no lack of forgiveness, no excommunication. Nothing like that! The sinner is just as much welcomed as the saint, because the sinner has come to be made a saint.

Jesus came to heal the sick, raise the dead, preach the gospel, and feed the hungry. Then this must be the will of God for man. God has no provision for death. "For I have no pleasure in the death of him that dieth, saith the Lord God: wherefore turn yourselves and live ye."[10]

This is the age when everyone must raise his concept of God until he has a God of one hundred percent love, in whom there is no evil, no punishment, no withholding, no death, no disease, no accidents, a God revealed by the Master: "I am come that they might have life and that they might have it more abundantly."[11] Was he speaking only to saints when he said that? No, he was speaking to anyone who could hear his voice: "I knock at the door of your consciousness. Open it and let me in, and then I will show you life abundant. I will not criticize you; I will not condemn you; I will not judge you. Who made me a judge over you? I will merely extend to you God's grace, which will lift you up, and you will never feel from my mind or my lips any condemnation."

### *The Consciousness of No Judgment Brings Peace*

Once we have experienced God we can never again judge, criticize, or condemn a person for anything he does. " 'Father, forgive them: for they know not what they do.'[12] If they only knew, they would live by Grace instead of by theft, but we will teach it to them, that is, we will teach it to those who are willing."

We cannot benefit anyone when we criticize, judge, condemn, or sit in judgment. The Master's whole ministry was one of love and forgiveness. It was not that he was so loving: it was because he was performing the ministry of his Father. And that is the mission given to us: not to sit in judgment, criticism, or condemnation, but to forgive, not caring what a person does tomorrow. If he wants to sin tomorrow and be punished again, that is his business, but this day he has come to us and received forgiveness. That is our mission and function.

## *Prayer as Communion*

Prayer becomes an attitude and an altitude when we begin to think about God as the soul of the universe, as that which sent it all into expression, that which does not withhold or punish and does not give just when we pray. Having released God from the nonsensical belief that He gives or withholds and having released Him from the need to exercise a miraculous power, since there is but the one power of God, our prayer now becomes the ability to commune within ourselves with this transcendental Presence which we know is the very Soul of our being.

Communion is a silence. It is not necessary for words to pass from us to God. God is already the all-knowing, and in our attitude of listening we are receptive and responsive to the presence and the power of God, to the will of God, to the way of God, and to the thoughts of God. Sometimes the still, small voice speaks; sometimes It thunders; but always when It speaks, the earth melts. And for It to speak does not necessarily mean using words because God can speak to us also in an inner warmth, a glow, a feeling of the Presence, an awareness of Something greater than human expression. That, of course, is the divine communion. We commune with God without voicing anything to God, without thinking any thoughts toward God, but instead our communion is more or less a listening attitude, and then gradually a melting into the one Consciousness.

In the daily living of the spiritual or mystical life, we must bear in mind that the object of that life is fulfillment. It is not to demonstrate anything; it is not to go any place; it is not to attain anything; it is not to achieve anything. The object of the spiritual life is to be fulfilled. We want only to be filled full of God. That is the object of our work—to live and move and have our being in God, of God, and through God. The whole function of the Infinite Way is fulfillment: fulfilling ourselves with the truth of God, with the love of God, the life of God, the spirit of God, and then letting all the other things and conditions be added unto us.

## Across the Desk

With the turn of the new year, we feel that we have a clean slate, a new start, a "putting off of the old man." Our resolutions are always filled with good intentions. But give us a few hours into the new year, and we find that "old man" hanging around. It isn't as easy as we had thought.

Paul gave us the secret—"If any man be in Christ, he is a new creature: old things are passed away; behold, all things are become new." How do we "be in Christ?" Practice consciously the principle of "I and my Father are one." As this principle begins to take over our life and live us, we experience the realization that the *I* is the Father and that this is what Jesus meant when explaining his Christhood.

In letting the *I* shine through us and live us each moment of the day through our practice, we suddenly find ourselves the "new creature." "Old things are passed away, and all things are become new." This has taken no human will power. We find our life transformed effortlessly by the Christ-Spirit within. Each moment is filled with newness, freshness, and joy-filled anticipation. Each hour fulfills the Christ-activity of the kingdom within. Each day embraces eternity. And thus the year is always new.

Tape Recorded Excerpts
Prepared by the Editor

Oftentimes students believe that the harmony and fulfillment of their present experience is limited by and sometimes
made impossible because of some act of omission or commission
in the past. They are held in the grip of karmic law which they
regard as irrevocable and irrefutable. In this new year and on this
new day, let us rise into that higher consciousness in which
karmic law does not operate. Then we are no longer the do-er,
but the beholder of God acting in us, as us, and through us.

Transcending Karmic Law

"As the world comes to us for help, it is a simple matter to
recognize the law of cause and effect operating, that whatever
the ill or discord, it is the result of a universal law. Then comes
our part in freeing them and being freed ourselves. . . . Even
though, as human beings, we are under the law, once we have
recognized the fact that we suffer only because it is the law, we
drop the law. . . and come out from the Old Testament into the
new Testament under Grace and Truth. And how do we do that?
Merely by recognizing that the law is not power: Grace and
Truth are power. Law operates only in belief. . . . Violation of
the law is only a belief. . . .

"You can bring yourself under Grace in this minute. . . .
Relinquish the desire for anything or anybody in the world in
the realization, 'I live by Grace, by the grace of God, not by the
grace of man.' . . . You have left the law and you have come
under Grace in the second that you are willing to say, 'I have no
external needs.' . . .

"You may have thought, heretofore, that Grace was something you sat around waiting for God to bestow upon you. No,
you do not have to wait for Grace. You can move out from

under the law this minute. Just relinquish your desires, and you are under Grace. You do not have to reach out physically or mentally for anything. The very moment you know that as an individual you are one with God, joint-heir with Christ in God, you can say, "Why, certainly I do not need anything or anybody. I live in my oneness with God." You are under Grace that minute.

"Only do not go back and sin again; do not go back tomorrow to a fear of lack, to a fear of sin, a fear of disease, or a fear of false appetite. Keep yourself living in the realization: 'Thank You, Father, I have no needs. The Father knows my needs. I leave it with the Father.' That is living by Grace. That is living by the Invisible, and you have moved out of the Old Testament into the New Testament. . . .

"Every patient that comes is under Mosaic law, the law of cause and effect. . . . In our treatment, we understand that he is no longer under the law but under Grace. That is how we free each other. I realize for you: You are not under the law. There is no law of cause and effect operating in this consciousness. There is only the law of divine grace in which you do 'not live by bread alone, but by every word that proceedeth out of the mouth of God.' . . . We hold each other in freedom by knowing that we are not under the law of karma, of cause and effect—not through former births or in births to come."

Joel S. Goldsmith, "Old Testament, the Law: Grace and Truth," *The First Steinway Hall Practitioner Class.*

"Every time an individual touches your consciousness and achieves any measure of freedom. . . your realization of divine grace has freed him from the effects of karmic law. Every time someone is freed from a disease from which he suffers through the violation of law, you have set him free through Grace. You have broken the law. Every time someone has sinned and, to human sense, is paying the penalty, and you bring the power of Grace to bear, you have set him free from the effects of his own sins through the power of Grace. . . .

"It is divine grace that sets a man free from the legal penalties. . . or from the physical penalties that are his due. . . . It is through Grace that these laws are set aside. . . . When people have come under the penalty for violating material law, . . . and spiritual realization has set them free, . . . Grace has transcended the law. The law came by Moses; the law is good for hu man beings. . . . Otherwise human beings. . . would not accept liberty: they would accept license.

"When you move out from the law, you should come under Grace, and you should forget those things which have passed: you should forget material law and legal law, . . . forget the sins of your past and the errors of your old ways, and be a new creature. . . . Do not carry your old selfhood around with you to remind yourself of the past. Today is a new day; today you are a new creature, born anew, born in Christ, spiritually conceived, immaculately conceived, spiritually maintained and sustained. Why talk and dig up all those errors of your past? . . . While you are under the law, it is foolish to believe that you can escape the penalty of it."

Joel S. Goldsmith, "The Result of Law Overcome Through Grace," *The First Steinway Hall Practitioner Class.*

# Chapter Two

# God and Prayer

And this is life eternal,
that they might know thee the only true God,
and Jesus Christ, whom thou hast sent.

John 17:3

To me that is the key to the whole of scripture. From Genesis to Revelation, scripture is trying to explain what God is, how to reach God, how to prepare for prayer, and how to pray to God.

First we must know what God is. Gradually the recognition unfolded to me that every idea of God I had was wrong because I had only an idea of God and certainly an idea is not God. Any concept of God that I entertain must be wrong because it is merely my concept. What can a concept be based upon, if not my own conditioning and limitation or somebody's imposed beliefs? Therefore, I cannot accept anybody's concept of God or anybody's belief in God. That God is, I know; the isness of God has never been a question in my mind.

If I say that God is Jesus Christ or that Jesus Christ is God,

I am certainly finitizing God, bringing It down to a human form, and casting out all the rest of the world that does not believe this, implying, "You poor beggars! You cannot come inside God's kingdom." If I think of God as a man with a big book that weighs our good and our evil, that, too, is a concept. Whether my ancestors formed that concept or whether I made it up in my own mind, it cannot be God. How could an infinite God fit into that limited concept?

### Is a Word in the Mind God?

God is spirit? You do not know what spirit is any more than I do. God is love? Neither do you know what love is any more than I do. Our human sense of love is not God. Do we know anything about love that does not have something to do with our relationships, whether at the marital, the parent-child, or the neighbor level? This is a human sense of love and cannot be God.

What is divine love? You have no answer. What is soul? You and I have no answer to that. We believe that we have a soul. But I do not know what soul is, nor do you, so again soul is a concept. If I say that God is truth, that is another concept, because we do not know what truth means. As a matter of fact, we get into serious trouble when we read that the Master said, "I am the way, the truth, and the life,"[1] because if we believe that, we must either accept a man as God, or we must realize that truth has a different meaning from our concept of it.

Years ago when a problem that seemed insoluble was presented to me, I sat in my office and I thought, "But there is a God, so there must be a solution. There is no such thing as an incurable disease. True, there are some diseases medically incurable, but that does not mean they are incurable: it just means that at the moment *materia medica* has not found a cure for that particular disease. Tomorrow it may, and then the disease will no longer be incurable. So it is incurable only to the ignorance existing in that area at the moment. There cannot be a problem that God cannot solve. Why then, can I not reach God? Why is not God doing something about this problem?"

Then I began to think about all that God is—mind, life, truth, love, soul, spirit—and finally out of the blue it struck me that if God were those things, why, right now I would have God and I would have harmony. But I do have mind, life, truth, love, soul, spirit, and yet I do not have harmony.

So I allowed a parade to go through my mind: God is love. Nothing happened. So that must be only a concept. Perhaps I have accepted this idea of God as love because that was John's concept. God is truth. That is some other person's concept, and I do not really know what it means.

I went through every synonym for God that I could possibly think of, and as I came to each one I recognized it to be a concept and not God. The further I went, the more I realized that no matter what word I used, it was a word in my mind. So ultimately I said to myself, "Is a word in my mind God?" And the answer must be, "No! Only God is God, and God cannot be finitized into a name, a description, or an analysis. God just *is.*"

## I *Reveals the Secret of God*

Then came the unfoldment that there is a word that is not a word in my mind. That word is *I.* I is not a word in my mind: I is my being; I is my identity. I is not a word I am thinking of; I is the thinker, not the thought. Regardless of any thought or concept of God, it cannot be God, because greater than any thought is the thinker. Is there anything greater than the thinker? Is not the source of thought the creator of thought? Then somewhere in the word *I* lies the secret of God. Moses said, "I Am that I Am,"[2] and Jesus taught, "I am the way, the truth, and the life.[3] . . . I will never leave thee, nor forsake thee.[4] . . . Lo, I am with you alway, even unto the end of the world.[5]. . . It is I; be not afraid."[6]

That day I made a tremendous advance toward the discernment of the secret of God as *I*. Then as the years went on, that word *I* began to define Itself, and I saw that it was really synonymous with Consciousness, because regardless of what I am, I must be consciousness. That must be the identity of *I*. Take Consciousness away, and is there an *I?* Take Consciousness away, and is there any awareness? Take Consciousness away, and is there form? All the form there is, is Consciousness formed. Is beauty anything but Consciousness formed as your idea of beauty? If you think of truth or if you think of love, is it not your consciousness of truth or of love that you are showing forth to the world? So love, life, and truth are forms of Consciousness, and the more illumined an individual is spiritually, the higher degree of love, truth, and life he will express.

### God As Individual Consciousness

Alongside the word *I*, the biggest word in the Infinite Way is *consciousness*. God is individual consciousness. God is individualized as you, and that is why the I of you has dominion and all the power of the *I* that is God. Jesus said that only the spirit of the Lord God upon him could give him power from on High. His last words to the disciples encouraged them to wait for that spiritual endowment: "Tarry ye in the city of Jerusalem, until ye be endued with power from on high,"[7] until the *I* of God is your *I,* until the consciousness of God is your consciousness.

The *I* which is God is individualized as the I which you are and which I am in our spiritual identity. The consciousness which God is, I am, for God is individualized as us. We are not a part of God, not just a speck of It. Each one of us is the allness of God made individually manifest. That allness of God appears as the quality and quantity of individual being.

### I Cannot Be Limited by a Body

God is neither "Lo here! or, Lo there! for, behold, the king-dom of God is within you."[8] But let us not be paganistic and believe that God is in the body—in the solar plexus or in the spinal cord—because that is finitizing God. Although we do believe that God is within us, that does not mean within our body. It means within us, and we are not body; we are something other than body.

There is only one exercise we use in the Infinite Way. That exercise not only gave me my full and complete revelation, but it showed me the secret of supply and completely changed my economic structure and enabled me to travel the world teaching the Infinite Way, and that without any memberships and without asking for contributions from anyone. It was the practice of going from the feet to the topmost hair of the head and discovering that I was not anywhere within that body. I walked along the street with this idea unfolding. I kept looking up and down my body, agreeing that I would not even want to believe that God could be encased in a finite form because we know that the infinity of God cannot be limited to a finite space. How could God or the son of God be confined in a corporeal body?

So I said to myself, "If I am not in this body, then, where am I? What am I? Who am I? And the word *I* struck fire. "Ah! There it is! 'I Am That I Am. . . I am the way, the truth, and the life. . . . I will never leave thee, nor forsake thee. . . . I will be with you unto the end of the world.'" That is not true of the body, is it? But it is true of I: I am incorporeal, I am spiritual, I am omnipresence in my real identity.

### Infinity Flows Through Conscious Oneness with the Source

God the Father is God the son, and all that God the Father is, God the son is, the son that must be raised up in us before we are spiritual man. As human beings we are not spiritual, but once the son of God is raised up in us, we are "joint-heirs."[9] If we are joint-heirs to all the heavenly riches, how are we going to claim our inheritance? The only way is to realize our oneness with the I-That-I-Am, and then let that Infinity flow. It will have Its own way of appearing outwardly, but you and I cannot tell how it is going to come.

I have taken whatever steps were necessary to see that Infinite Way books are made available to the public, but I could not put them in your possession. If I had mailed you one without your seeking or asking for it, it would have gone on your bookshelf. Only the Father, the *I,* could go before me to "make the crooked places straight"[10] and bring these books into your possession.

When I was given this work to do, I was told never to seek a student. Why? Because all I would get would be a lot of human beings, and most of them would throw stones at me. If I tried to tell anyone that God is inseparable and indivisible from man, he would not listen to me  and certainly would not read a book I might send him. But if some spiritual opening in him leads him to the book, that is not Joel, but the *I,* operating independently of human will, human desire, or human effort.

The *I* which is God is the *I* which we are, inseparable and indivisible. That *I* could not be the relationship of one man to God, for God could not operate to do something for one person and leave all the rest out in the cold. Whatever God is, that is what God is to all being. There is no such think as any one group, such as the Hebrews, being the chosen people of God. Israel, yes, if we think of Israel as the spiritually illumined, then we are not limiting it to the Hebrews. Buddha, yes, if we are thinking of Buddha as meaning the enlightened one. Then Buddha is the son of God; Christ is the son of God; Melchizedek is the son of God. In other words, the spiritually illumined consciousness is the son of God.

### *God's Grace Given to Everyone*

When we come into the awareness of our allness, that is when we begin to realize:

"I can of mine own self do nothing,"[11]
so I sit down and am
instructed of God.
God is my own consciousness,
and I draw forth from my consciousness
what God has stored up for me,
all the dominion and
the grace God has given me.

Many persons misunderstand the word *grace* and thereby lose their whole life's demonstration. They think that grace is a favor God does for somebody. But is not God's grace incarnate in every individual, including the animals and the birds, awaiting recognition? What is ours is ours by reason of God's grace, and there is no way to find God's grace by going to church, being baptized, or taking communion. Too many people have been baptized and had the benefit of everything they can get from ceremony and ritual, and yet they are still subject to sin, disease, and death. If God's grace were not on earth before there was a church, there is no God. We do know, however, that God's grace was here, is here, and always will be here, whether men avail themselves of it or not.

The secret of the mystical revelation is that God constitutes individual being. God-consciousness and individual consciousness are one and the same. Individual consciousness, however, has been conditioned by human life in such a way that some persons believe that first and last they are Hebrews, some that they are Christians, some that they are Buddhists, and some that they are Mohammedans. Such beliefs arise out of a state of conditioning, but despite that conditioning, everybody is a child of God, and if all religions were done away with, man would still be the child of God.

The only God there is, is *I*. That is the only thing that is not a projected image; that is the projector of all the images, but it is not projected. *I* contains the secret of God. *I* to be *I* must be Consciousness, so *I* and Consciousness are one and the same. If we see that *I*, that Consciousness, is an infinity that individualizes Itself as our consciousness, we do not have to go anywhere but to our consciousness, turn within and say, "Father illumine me, enlighten me."

When we are so high in consciousness that our attitude is purely a listening for the voice of God, we are in an attitude and an altitude of prayer, and the voice of God which is always speaking is then heard.

Only knowing God aright will make possible the efficacious prayer that results in signs following. We all agree that God is the all-knowing, but do we agree on that when in prayer we tell God what we would like and almost what day of the week we would like it? The prayer that says, "God, send me daily bread," meaning food, clothing, and housing, or the prayer that pleads, "Oh, God, heal my child," are both insults to God, because we are really saying, "God, I know You do not know this, but I am telling it to You." Are we not thereby presuming that we are greater than omniscience? What nonsense! Either God is omniscient, or we might as well begin to search for another God. But if God is omniscient, we never dare to go to God with a wish, a desire, a hope, a request, or any attempt to influence Him, only an "Illumine me; enlighten me; speak to me; reveal Thy will to me, Thy wish, Thy plan," but never in the sense of "God, heal Mrs. Jones' child," or "Oh, God, you know that these poor suffering people are good people, and they ought to have food," or any of the traditional prayers heard daily in a house of worship. Such prayers are virtually telling God His business and accusing

Him of not having enough love or enough power to take care of
our needs.

### Prayer, a Listening Attitude

And behold, the Lord passed by,
and a great and strong wind rent the mountains,
and broke in pieces the rocks before the Lord;
but the Lord was not in the wind:
and after the wind an earthquake;
but the Lord was not in the earthquake:

And after the earthquake a fire; but the Lord was
not in the fire: and after the fire a still small voice.
I Kings 19:11,12

God-power is made evident in our experience only in proportion as our prayer becomes a listening attitude. Prayer is an
attitude, and prayer is an altitude of consciousness. But even the
highest mystical prayer can be prefaced by some thoughts and
statements on our part, such as:

"I and my Father are one."[12]
I sit here to hear the "still small voice,"
to receive the conscious awareness of God's grace
that I may be instructed and illumined.

We may think along that line until we settle down into a
quietness, and all of a sudden come to a stillness. Then we are
in mystical prayer: we are thinking no thoughts and speaking no
words, only acknowledging that God is not in the problem but
in the still small voice.

When we experience the still small voice, we have reached
God. When "he uttered his voice, the earth melted"[13]—the earth

of evil. Nothing real melts; God's earth does not melt, just the earth, which Jesus called "this world."[14] This world with its beliefs and concepts will melt, and His kingdom will be revealed.

We may take the word *omniscience* into our preparatory period for prayer:

> God is omniscience, the all-knowing.
> God is responsible for me
> because God is the creator of my being.
> Therefore God knows of my existence,
> and neither life nor death can separate me
> from the life of God or the love of God.
> So here I am waiting
> for omniscience to declare Itself.

When we have lived with God as omniscience long enough, the life of prayer becomes so automatic that the moment a problem presents itself, we just close our eyes, open our ears, and then a deep breath comes, "Ah, God is on the field," and we do not have to give any more thought to the problem.

### *God As Omnipotence Releases Us from any Desire for God To Do Anything*

How many hymns have been sung and how many words have been written about omnipotence! But there is scarcely a soul who sings about omnipotence or talks about it who believes it, because to almost everyone omnipotence means a mighty power over other powers. But that is not omnipotence. "Omni" means all. To know God aright means to know God as omnipotence, and that means never to pray for God to do anything to anybody or to anything, because in the realm of omnipotence there is nothing for God to do anything about. Omnipotence is always the all and only power.

What about the power of sin, disease, death, lack, limitation, and man's inhumanity to man? These are power only to those who accept them as power or who accept God as a power over something.

We do not pray for God to destroy our enemy or to heal disease. That is the mistake made by prayer groups or by persons who are praying to God to heal Mrs. Jones. Not for a minute can we believe that God leaves Mrs. Jones unhealed until someone intercedes for her. God is not leaving the world in trouble, waiting for someone to get holy and ask Him to correct the situation.

If we have a God of omniscience, we refrain from trying to influence Him. With a God of omnipotence, we can release God and stop looking to Him to do something. We do not pray to God to have the sun come up in the morning or to have the sun go down at night. No, we know that God appearing in the form of the operation of nature governs all phenomena of nature.

Some persons, however, mistakenly speak to God and say, "God, You do not know that Mr. Jones is hungry, Mrs. Brown is poor, and Mrs. Smith is sick, so I am begging and pleading with You to do something for them." As a matter of fact, why should God? Why encourage a person to pray to God for something without first sufficiently enlightening him that he will not get any answer unless he changes?

## Preparation To Receive God's Grace

There must be a fitness to receive the things of God. When a person reaches the point where he cries out, "Oh, Christ cleanse me, purify me"—not "Christ, save me from being killed"—that is the preparation for forgiveness. That is what happened to the woman taken in adultery who received God's grace after she had given up her adulterous ways and had obviously so reached the end of the road that she pleaded, "Oh, Christ!" Then her sins were forgiven.

The thief on the cross received God's grace because he was reaching out for the Christ. If he had reached out for the Christ and Jesus had not been there, somebody else would have been, because no one can seriously want to be purified or made whole without the Christ appearing as a man, a woman, a book, a teacher, or a teaching. If none of those is available, somebody will be raised up to let the person reaching out know that something closer to him than breathing will release him. Why? The spirit of God is in him. There is no spirit of God separate from the spirit of man.

In the absolute sense, God is omnipresent, but God is only omnipresent as the consciousness of individual being. Therefore, if there is one person in a room with a consciousness of God, no evil can happen in that room, more especially if the others are at all attuned. God is the spirit of man, and therefore, the only place that we can bring God-power into expression is from within ourselves. That is where It is. It is not floating about in a room, but It is in any room as the consciousness of man where It is realized. Without this acknowledgment and reliance, however, It does not function.

In some of my deep meditations I have seen the soul of man as if it were a tiny, closed-up bud. As I have worked with students or patients over a period of time, I have watched this opening, just like a rosebud coming into full bloom, and their whole nature changes. Because they had no access to God before, they could not receive the things of God, but now they can. There must be a God-faculty in order to receive the things of God; there must be a means of Its entrance into our consciousness.

We must *know* the truth for the truth to make us free. Everything comes through consciousness, and if we are not conscious of God's presence, we do not have It. If we are not conscious of God's power, we do not have It. If we are not conscious of God's omniscience, we do not have It. Therefore, anything that comes to us must come through our consciousness.

### *"Turn Yourselves, and Live Ye"*

"In all thy ways acknowledge him.[15]. . . And ye shall know the truth, and the truth shall make you free."[16] When we begin to live in this atmosphere, we make way for the grace of God to flow through us. It cannot flow through those of us who are living as human beings. There must be a fitness; there must be a turning. We must be willing for our nature to change. "For I have no pleasure in the death of him that dieth, said the Lord God: wherefore turn yourselves, and live ye."[17]

People come to us with all their problems, and they are filled with hate, envy, jealousy, bigotry, and bias, and yet they expect the grace of God to flow through them. Can God flow in any way except through love, and did not Jesus show us what he meant by love? "Thou shalt love thy neighbor as thyself."[18] If you say you love God whom you have not seen, and you do not love man whom you have seen, you are a liar. "Inasmuch as ye did it not to one of the least of these, ye did it not to me."[19] Why? Because I am you, and what I do of good unto you, I have done unto the Christ of myself. What I do of evil to anyone, I have done unto myself, and it must react more upon me than upon him.

How can we be instruments through which God can work, if the quality of our being is not love? Love is the secret of the spiritual life—not human love. Human love tells us to send our children to college; spiritual love demands that we save out some of what we have for the child down the street who cannot afford it, but who also wants to go to college. Human love tells us to support our family, but spiritual love requires us also to remember the family down the street that is still struggling for a livelihood. Human love says that the man in prison is none of our business; he got himself there. Divine love says, "I was in prison, and ye came unto me."[20]

The Master has shown us what is expected of us in order

that we may be sons of God and receive the grace of God. I do not decry rituals that may be helpful to some persons. In fact, I am just as holy when I am sitting in a chair, but there are times when I must go to my knees. Perhaps it is a sense of humility that drives me there to show me my nothingness. When I am in a big city, very often I walk into a church because I want the quiet and the peace of that sanctuary. I do not care what church it is as long as it has an open door. When the urge is there, it is not important which church we go into. Any church will be quiet and give us a physical sense of peace. But if there is a minister in that church who has been ordained of God, there will be such a holy atmosphere that we will be healed by just going in and sitting there.

### A Change of Consciousness
### Is All-Important

The healings we may bring to people are not the important thing. What is important is that those persons stay with us long enough to have a change of consciousness. "Turn yourselves, and live ye." If there is not a transformation, all the physical, mental, emotional, or financial healings that a person receives will prove to be of only temporary value. Every spiritual treasure that we lay up becomes a blessing tomorrow, next year, or the year after. As we visit those in prison, comfort those who mourn, feed the hungry, and clothe the naked, we are laying up spiritual treasures—especially if we tell no man about it.

This does not mean that the secretary or the minister will not know about the check you mail, but do not let your neighbor next door know; do not let it be broadcast to the world if you can help it. The things that God sees in secret are rewarded openly because I and the divine consciousness, individualized as me, are one. What goes on in my consciousness determines my life, not what someone thinks of me, and not whether someone likes me or not. What affects my life is my relationship with God, my relationship with my Self, and if I keep myself under the law of God, I will receive my reward from God.

"Lean not unto thine own understanding.[21]. . . Whither shall I go from thy spirit?"[22] Omnipresence, omnipotence, omniscience: it is all there. It is the activity of the Christ, the spirit of God in man, that ultimately will save him from mortality. That mortality will be put off, not by humanly wanting to put it off, but as the spirit of God touches man inside and puts it away.

### Across The Desk

In this Letter dealing with prayer from the highest standpoint, it is quite appropriate that I should [talk about] a book by Joel on this important subject — *The Altitude Prayer.*[23]

This is a book culled from Joel's most significant work on the subject of prayer which will go far toward opening consciousness to "the effectual fervent prayer of a righteous man which availeth much." It is the kind of book that will be of interest, not only to Infinite Way students, but to all seekers for a deeper awareness of God.

### *Living Between Two Worlds*
a review by Louise B. Wilson[1]

A Review of *Living Between Two Worlds,* by Joel S. Goldsmith, edited by Lorraine Sinkler. [Acropolis Books, Atlanta, 1996.]

In Joel Goldsmith's first book, *The Infinite Way,* originally published in 1947, he answers the question: How does one set about attaining spiritual consciousness and thereby lose material sense?

In his more recent book, Goldsmith says that since God is Spirit, the only world is a spiritual world, and the only man is spiritual man. The proof of that is that through the development of spiritual discernment we are able to see the world as it is, to see the materialistic concept evaporate and in its place behold a world of harmony.

As we work with this approach we give more power to God and less to the external world. It is here that our search begins. During the search we are living between two worlds: the world of material sense in which we give power to persons, things and conditions, and the world of spiritual awareness where we begin to believe there is Something greater than the external powers of evil.

The ability to move from the world of material sense into the world of spiritual discernment is proportionate to our ability to close our eyes to the appearance and wait for that inner intuition, the voice of God, to reveal to us the truth of what we are beholding.

We constantly live between the world of appearances and the world of spiritual grace, the world of fear and the world with no fear, the world of mind and body and the world of soul. We are constantly trying to live in this world and not be of it.

Since my introduction to Goldsmith through his book *The Thunder of Silence* in 1961, I have read all his books and I listen to his tapes regularly. I feel that he teaches what early Friends experienced and even though the terminology may vary, the truth that is being revealed is the same. As Friends, we can benefit by his teachings if we are willing to work with the principles by living them in our daily lives.

The foundation of the Infinite Way rests on obtaining the experience of the Presence. The principles set forth in *Living Between Two Worlds* are the same as in all his work: God is appearing as individualized being, as you and me; we must live in the Now; God is; and throughout his writing Goldsmith shares his experiences in the ever expanding realization of "I and the Father are one."

To read a book by Goldsmith is just the beginning. If the

words find no place in you, put the book down; if the words do find a place in you, you will not be able to put the book down. You will begin to want the words to become flesh, and as you work with the principles you will gradually see a change in your relationship with others and your own feelings and thoughts.

The process is slow. It may be a long time between the day you read that God is supply and supply appears as health, position, money, home, education, vacation, etc., and the day you realize that God is supply.

In his new book, Goldsmith touches me at my center and confirms what is already there. He speaks of the power of silence and the need for prayer and meditation. He reminds us that as we practice the presence of God an inner stillness and peace come which leads to wholeness. In all his teaching you are led within, to the one and only Teacher.

My inner life has been deepened by the experience of making conscious union with God. He has also helped me to see that our consciousness externalizes as our world. What we see "out here" is what we are within. We begin to realize that we are not in the world: the world is in us.

To read *Living Between Two Worlds* can be the beginning of our realization that God in the midst of us makes us heirs to the kingdom. To recognize our divine sonship, Goldsmith says that we must once again accept our dominion and this means that we create our own world. The book will lead us to the Christ within and help us to bear witness to Him.

[1]Reprinted by permission from *Quaker Life*
(Richmond, Indiana, Friends United Press). September 1974.

*Chapter Three*

# "Now I See"

Until the importance of knowing God aright is understood there is little use of attempting to learn anything further. Knowing God means not merely knowing God intellectually, that is, through the mind, but so well that a person could almost say, "Whereas I was blind, now I see."[1] To understand the nature of God, the three words omniscience, omnipotence, and omnipresence need to be indelibly impressed on consciousness, for without the fullest understanding of their meaning, a student can never approach God. Serious students might benefit greatly by looking up the meaning of these three words in an unabridged dictionary so as to get a more comprehensive understanding of them.

## *Omniscience*

Hymns are sung to the all-wise God, and people are always claiming that God is the all-knowing. But what happens the next minute? They tell God they have a pain; they tell God the rent is due or that they need employment. In that instant they deny God, just as much as if they were to say, "I do not believe there is an all-knowing God." If they knew God to be the all-knowing, would they ever go to God with any problem? Would they ever go to God to try to influence Him in their behalf? No, once a student grasps the nature of God as omniscience, he can never again reach up to God or even dream of asking God for peace on earth or for anything else.

Students of the Infinite Way should spend a great deal of time working with the principle of God as omniscience. This principle cannot be learned in two weeks, two months, or two years. How long it will take students to come to the point where they never are tempted to tell God anything, to try to influence God, or to let God know about the problem, I do not know.

Eventually you as a student must get to the place where this is so much a part of your consciousness that when anyone asks you to pray for him to attain some end, inwardly you would be laughing and thinking: What do you mean by "pray for you"? Shall I tell God that you need good health tomorrow or supply? Should I tell God to overcome your enemies or change your disposition? Do you see how ridiculous it all sounds when it is put this way? But that response is possible only because in some measure God has become so real as omniscience that you cannot imagine going into prayer or meditation in any other way than by just closing the eyes and listening because you have nothing to tell God.

### Becoming Instruments for the Voice of God

What must be your attitude of prayer? To hear the voice of God. God is not in the whirlwind: God is in the "still small voice."[2] Do you want God? Then, according to scripture, the only way to get God is to listen until you hear that still small voice. Our attitude must be: "Speak, Lord; for thy servant heareth,"[3] not Thy servant has something to tell You or ask You, not that Your servant wants favors, but that Your servant wants to hear Your voice.

If you ever hear the voice of God, if you ever receive an impartation within, if you ever feel an inner release because of God's presence, you will not be afraid of a lion, a storm, or a flood. What can come near your dwelling place if you have God at the center of your being and are on such good terms with Him that He speaks to you?

Does this not make it clear why there is no room in the Infinite Way for egotism? We cannot heal; we cannot protect; we cannot enrich. We can only be instruments through which the voice of God comes, and that makes us very humble because we know that we can of our own selves do nothing. We never will be so spiritual that we can be anything except transparencies through which the voice of God can speak. For a teacher or practitioner to believe that he is ever going to become so spiritual as to have spiritual power is immediately to defeat himself. The further he goes, the more of a transparency he becomes, but that will be because, in his nothingness, he no longer speaks to God or tries to influence or use God. He has learned enough to be a clean windowpane to let the light shine through.

If you work with the nature of God as omniscience, sooner or later, if you are faithful, your nature will so change that you will never even be tempted to tell God anything or to get God to do anything. Your new attitude will always be keeping your ear open. Whatever you are doing—giving a lecture, teaching, or painting a house—you will never do anything without your ear being partially open, listening for that voice, which when It comes will melt the whole earth of error. With that one word alone, omniscience, you will be less of a human being and more the son of God who is always attentive to the Father.

### Omnipotence Eliminates All Other Powers

Omnipotence is the next word that must become an integral part of your being. There are few persons in all the world who really believe that God is omnipotent. Not even the com-posers who have written hymns to an omnipotent God or the ministers who keep talking about the omnipotence of God fifty-two weeks a year believe it. True, they pay lip service to it.

But if you spend a few weeks or months with the nature of God as omnipotence and get the realization of it, what will you ever need God-power for after that? Will there be any other power to take to God to be overcome, risen above, or destroyed, if God is omnipotent? If you catch the nature of God as omnipotence, can you ever again ask God to do anything, or even expect it? If God could come down to your level of thought, He might say, "Well, what is this power that you want Me to do something about? The power of sin, the power of dis-ease, the power of lack? If they are powers, then *I* am not omnipotent, so how do you know *I* am strong enough for the job? But if *I* am omnipotent, you do not need *My* power, because there is no other power."

You cannot imagine what an understanding of this will do for you. Somebody comes to you with a need, and instantly it must come to you, "Can it be a power? That takes away from God's omnipotence, so then not only cannot God do anything about it, but neither can I."

In some degree, everybody gives power to negative forces, such as bullets and atomic bombs, or germs. None of these has power except the power that universal belief gives them. The truth of that statement has been proved in the last hundred years every time a person has gone to a spiritual teacher or prac-titioner with just a simple cold and through the practitioner's knowing God's omnipotence has been healed of it. Had the cold been a power in the first place it could not have been healed. The practitioner did not do any of the things considered neces-sary to destroy the cold or flu germs. All he did was know God's omnipotence, which correctly interpreted means the non-power of the germ theory. If the cold is healed, then to that extent, it has been proved that it was not power.

Infection from cuts, bruises, and boils have been proved to be of no power. In the past hundred years, Christian Science, Unity, New Thought, and Infinite Way practitioners have, through their handling of tens of thousands of cases of blisters, burns, cuts, and bruises, proved that infection is not a power. They have not proved that God healed those things and other conditions because of a metaphysician. "God is no respecter of persons,"[4] so why should He do it for a metaphysician and not for a non-metaphysician? What God will not do for a non-metaphysician he will not do for a metaphysician. God works through law, so it is not God that heals infections. It is knowing the truth: "Ye shall know the truth and the truth shall make you free."[5] The truth is that infections, germs, beliefs, and theories are not power. God has not healed these cases, in fact, God has never healed any case and never will.

### The Illumined Consciousness Knows the Truth

Healing comes through the illumined consciousness of an individual, and it must be illumined to the extent of an understanding of the real meaning of omniscience and omnipotence. That is the only illumined consciousness there is. Illumination is not seeing visions or having emotional experiences. The illumined consciousness is the consciousness that knows the truth, and the Infinite Way teaches that there is no truth to be known about man. The only truth to be known is the truth about God. If you understand omniscience and omnipotence, you have enough truth to change your life and the lives of all those who come to you, once you have worked with these words long enough so that they are not merely intellectual knowledge but actual awareness.

In Russian mysticism there is what is called the prayer of Jesus. It is taught that if this prayer is voiced over and over again, never less than three or four hundred times a day, seven days a week, and never less than fifty-two weeks a year, eventually that prayer goes from the head into the heart, and from then on a person never again has to say it: he listens, and it comes up to him. In one sense that is similar to the Infinite Way teaching that after a person learns the letter of truth, really learns it so that he understands omniscience and omnipotence, and then works with those words until they go from the head to the heart, not repeating them parrot-like but contemplating their inner meaning, then when someone asks his help, he smiles, and his smile is only his outer response to the truth that is coming up from deep inside.

No one who has not come to the conviction of God as omniscience and omnipotence will ever go very far in developing a healing consciousness. It may take a year, five years, or ten years to reach the place where you never have to wonder what the truth is that you have to know. I can tell you about omnipotence and omniscience but the important thing for you is to understand them spiritually.

Anyone who catches the significance of omnipresence is automatically freed from fear of any nature. The only reason you have to fear is if you are not in the presence of God because then that puts the responsibility for your life upon you. What can you do about this? Whether on a battle front or in a city with contagion or an epidemic, what can you do about it, if you are there alone? On the other hand, what can any of these beliefs do if God is there with you?

## The Importance of Repetition

After studying Infinite Way writings, students will discover how repetitious I can really be with one idea. For example, take the statement, "The place where I stand is holy ground. Where God is, I am; where I am, God is, because we are inseparably one." Count how many times that idea appears in Infinite Way writings. And why? Telling you once that God is omnipresence, and that God is present where you are may be teaching it to you, but that is no guarantee that you are learning it.

Only when it is drilled into your consciousness day after day, week after week, month after month will something inside of you explode and you will exclaim, "Oh, God is here"; or you will hear inside of you, "I will never leave you, nor forsake you." Then you will understand the reason for all these quotations and all the repetition in the writings. Is it not like the child who wants nothing more than the assurance of his parent's presence? What more could you possibly want than the assurance of God's presence? What could a bullet do if God were present? Is a bullet more than God? Is a bomb more than God? God is omnipotent. Omnipotence, omniscience, and omnipresence keep volleying back and forth, supporting one another, so that you can live your whole life with those three words.

### New Light on the Nature of Error

After you understand the omniscience, omnipotence, and omnipresence of God comes the second important unfoldment which is on the nature of error. Go back over what you have read in this letter and see if without ever mentioning it I have not already included the nature of error. In the face of omnipotence, what is the nature of error? Non-power! In the face of omniscience, what is the nature of error? Non-intelligence! In the face of omnipresence, what is the nature of error? Non-presence! In fact, in these three words are included the nature of God and the nature of error. But in working with them, you have to remember consciously that you have just handled the nature of error.

Most persons who come into metaphysics like to talk about the omnipotence of God, Its omniscience and omnipresence, but they do not thereby rule out the presence and power of something else. They have the full circle only when they realize consciously the nature of error as nonpresence, nonpower, non-intelligence, and without any law to maintain it.

As you develop the consciousness of omniscience, you recognize at the same moment that this precludes the possibility of error having law, intelligence, substance, or activity. When you are living omnipotence and then realize that omnipotence means the non-power of any form of error, evil, or threat, and also that the realization of omnipresence automatically means the nonpresence of the appearance, you have brought the three into one and you have the whole.

### The Law of God
### Is Forever in Operation

One of the reasons for the lack of healing is the belief that God is going to do something to the error. So you are waiting for something that cannot happen; you are waiting for a God-power to do something. That not only is a barrier to healing work, but patients, who unconsciously accept this, stand in the way of their being healed, because all the time you are presenting truth to them, they are sitting around waiting for God to walk on the face of the water and do something. God is not going to walk on the face of the water or do anything, and the belief that God is proves that a person does not know the name or nature of God.

When a seed is planted, nature does not start to do something. Before the seed is put into the ground, the law of nature is in operation, only there is no seed for it to operate on. But when you put the seed in the ground, the law that is already there goes to work. There is no law sitting off to the side waiting for you to put the seed in the ground and then begin to go to work. No, the law of God is omnipresent, therefore it cannot begin to be present now. You cannot bring God into action. It is not your prayers that bring God-power: the God-power is omnipresent, and your prayer is but the connecting link.

It is like turning on your radio. Simply turning it on does not create any program. By turning it on you merely tune in to the program already in progress. So it is that anyone waiting for God to do something is wasting his time. God is not going to do anything a minute from now. Whatever God is going to do, God is doing, and God has been doing since the beginning of time. You cannot start or inaugurate a God-action. Nothing will do that. Being good will not do it; reforming will not do it; being moral will not do it; tithing will not do it. You cannot set God into action: God is omnipresent. But you can close your eyes to the appearance and tune in.

To know this is to know something about the nature of God that the world as a whole does not know. The universal belief is that if you pray to God, God answers, but with so many unanswered prayers we know this cannot be. Nothing man can do will influence God—not being good, not being moral, not reforming, not being charitable. But what they will do is to bring you into at-onement with the law of God with which you are not at-one when you are being bad, unkind, or uncharitable.

That is why at some period a person has to stop long enough to tune in to God, and then his badness is turned into goodness. He does not stop being bad and become good because he does not have that power; he does not even have the power to lose his ignorance about God and turn it to wisdom about God. All he has the power to do is to stop whatever he is doing or thinking and tune in. God will make him good and God will enlighten him, because of omnipresence. The power of God is there whenever a person tunes in to It. Therefore, omnipresence, omnipotence, and omniscience must constantly be the aim of his realization.

Any sinner can contact God. He has only to stop long

enough to tune in and desire God. That is all it takes! And then he experiences the omnipresent activity of the Christ. The Christ is present whenever a person reaches out for It. This does not mean that Jesus is present. The moment anyone reaches out, the Christ is present, either invisibly or visibly in some form.

### God Knows the Intents of the Heart

Only through prayer do you have contact with God. The question must have arisen in your mind: How shall I pray? Certainly by now the need for any words or thoughts to explain to God what you need has been taken away from you. There is nothing you can think or say that is going to reach God. What will do it? Motive! The total efficacy of prayer can be summed up in the one word *motive*. If God is omniscience, God must know what is in your heart, so what is the use of going to God and saying, "God, make me pure," when that is not what you mean at all. It is far better to go to God without words and without thoughts, but with the inner motive, "God, You know the workings of my heart. Reward me accordingly." If your motive is not right, you will get an awful wallop. If your motive is merely, "Make me well," or "Make me prosperous," or "Make me happy," there will be no answer, because "My kingdom is not of this world."[6] *My* kingdom is spiritual. So if you go to God, you must go wanting spiritual grace and forget what you seem to need in the human picture because you cannot reach God while that is your primary goal.

If you believe in omniscience, the only way you can reach God is to close your eyes, realizing, "I cannot tell You anything, but You search the heart, the marrow, and the intents of the mind, God, You know me. Here I am." As long as your motive is to receive God's wisdom, God's voice, God's presence, something of a spiritual nature that has no relationship to your human world, It will adjust your human world. *It* will adjust it, not you. You cannot decide what you want, with one exception. The moment you have awakened to the fact that you need God or you need truth, then you can have the desire to go where God or the truth is to be found or revealed.

It is true that a person can attain the realization of God as omnipresence by himself without any outside help from books or teachers, but he might have to take thirty-five or more years to accomplish it. From 1909 on I was searching inside myself, and twenty years later it happened. So if time is not an element, you can do it all by yourself. Remember, too, that although the kingdom of God is within you, you will find it only if your motive is pure.

## Prayer Must Contain Nothing
### of a Selfish Nature

If you want God for some purpose of your own, it will not work because the nature of God is such that God does not give anybody anything for himself. No person receives the revelation of God unless the receiving of that revelation will enable him to go out and preach the gospel, feed the hungry, heal the sick, or in some way serve a constructive purpose. God never does anything just for you or for me. God never reveals the truth to you or to me for your profit or mine, or for your help or mine. You have no understanding of the nature of God if you believe that God does anything for anybody's personal benefit. Therefore, while God is omnipresence and ready to be revealed, you cannot receive the revelation because you are open only to the extent of receiving God for yourself, and thus you have closed the door.

If you want God, you must want God for whatever the consequences may be, and if God tells you to leave mother, father, sister, and brother, then that is what you are to do. But be sure it is God revealing this to you and not your human mind or will operating. If God tells you to give up your business, you must do it. You cannot do it because you would like to do it; you cannot do it because that is your preference. In going to God there has to be a pure motive, and that pure motive is not to get something for you or for your family.

Prayer is a farce if it contains anything of a personal, selfish, or exclusive nature. The words on your lips and the thoughts in your mind sometimes are the very barriers to your prayers, because you are lying to yourself and you are lying to God. You cannot lie to God, because God searches the "joints and marrow, and is a discerner of the thoughts and intents of the heart."[7] Therefore, it is far better to forget all words and thoughts, and go to God saying, "God how can I fool You? Here I am. Fill me." Do you see that? Then you have a much better chance to receive God's grace.

### All Principles of the
### Infinite Way Are Interlocking

Today there are teachers and there are teachings, so there really is no need to wait twenty years or more to get an answer. If you open yourself to the Christ, the Christ will somehow meet your need, and it can very well be through a book, a teaching, or a teacher. Remember always that these are but the instruments. The purpose of a book, a teacher, or a teaching is to reveal the nature of God to you, so that you yourself can make your contact.

Prayer, the nature of God, and the nature of error are all interlocking. One leads to the other. When you are finished, it is a circle. Through your understanding of omniscience, omnipotence, and omnipresence, you automatically see the nature of error. When you see the nature of error, instead of wasting time fighting it or praying to God to do something about it, you are able to sit quietly and listen, and you are in prayer.

You will not reach God without prayer, because even when you know the nature of God and the nature of error, if you do not attain that inner stillness that enables you to hear the still small voice, it is not complete: you have only knowledge up in the head. Without knowledge in the head, however, you will not get the inner peace to enable you to pray aright. It is all interlocking. You need the letter of truth as a raft; you need it as a means to an end. But no matter how much of the letter you have, if you do not go to the next step and let that lead you to the Spirit, the awareness or the consciousness, you cannot complete your work.

If you were praying for someone, no matter how much truth you know and include in your prayer, be sure that you conclude with the meditation, "Now, God, I did not say any of this for Your benefit. This was all for my benefit, so I could get still inside, but now it is Your turn. I am prepared to be still. I am listening."

## ACROSS THE DESK

From time to time in the letter this year, there will be a special section devoted to teaching the Infinite Way, material taken from Joel's recorded work. While most of those who will read the letter may never be teachers of this work, this does not mean that such a section is only for persons who fall into that category. You will find that the material is exceedingly practical for all students and helpful to them in their spiritual unfoldment. So I heartily recommend a thorough study of this material, knowing what rich fruitage it will yield in your experience.

Easter comes early this year, at the end of the month. May it mark a time of renewal and restoration for you as it is for all nature. Rise now out of the tomb of material sense into the discernment of the spiritual universe here and now, always everpresent but only awaiting your discovery and awareness.

## TEACHING THE INFINITE WAY

"Teachers of the Infinite Way are at the same time narrowly confined and completely free. It is a paradox. Unless they stick to the subject of the nature of God, the nature of error, and the nature of prayer, the teaching is not going to complete its function. The minute they stray outside those three subjects, they are outside the Infinite Way. On the other hand, Infinite Way teachers have unlimited freedom because there are hundreds of different ways of presenting those subjects, and nobody to tell them how, what, why, or when. They are on their own and must be led by inner guidance as to when it is wise to say a certain thing or to hold it back. *The substance of Infinite Way teaching must be within the framework of the nature of God, the nature of error, and the nature of prayer.*

"There is no way for a student or patient to be set free except as he gains his freedom through an understanding of God. Otherwise the student is left with the belief that God may punish or reward, that is, if he does something to please God he will reap a rich reward, and if he tithes that will make God loosen up. It must be conveyed to the student that there is no way on earth to influence God and that nothing he or anyone else can do will gain God's favor. The student can refrain from smoking and drinking; he can refrain from sex; he can refrain from eating meat; he can go on month-long fasts; but he cannot move God. Unless he understands that about God, he will always be making an effort to please God.

"On the other hand, if he is not preparing his consciousness for the flow of God, he is not going to receive God's grace. The Master's ministry was always addressed to a 'you'; you must forgive seventy times seven; you must pray for your enemy; you must love your neighbor as yourself; you must seek the kingdom of God and His righteousness; you must not judge after appearances. That brings the Christ-ministry down to you and me—

not to God but to you and me. Until we are fit transparencies, the omnipresence that is always there cannot function, just as a pane of glass that is dirty cannot be a clear transparency for light, and if it gets dirty enough, it will shut out the light entirely.

"The first cleansing that must come about is the desire to know God aright. If it is intense enough, sometimes just that one desire will make all of the rest take place in a hurry. But without that intense desire to know God, there is no way to bring about the cleansing process. We could read books of spiritual literature all day and all night, and perhaps if we had a hundred years, that reading might gradually and slowly cleanse us.

"Students must understand the nature of God as omniscience, omnipotence, and omnipresence. God is just as much here and now as is the fresh air, but available only in proportion to our knowing, applying, and living the truth. Instead of searching for an omnipresent God, we acknowledge God, omnipresent, close our eyes and listen.

"As a teacher working with beginners, you probably would take only one of these three words for a lesson: Omniscience for the first lesson, omnipotence for the second, and omnipresence for the third, followed by the nature of error as a natural sequence in the next lesson and prayer in the lesson after that. Use the sixth lesson for review to tie them all together.

"Those of you who are teaching should not go on to other subjects until you are sure that the student or the class has caught the importance of these first six lessons. Then, six months later you should go through one or two hours of review of those first lessons, because it is easy for students to forget these principles and to lose them.

"The only time you can be sure that students will not lose what they have been taught is after they have had the demonstrable realization with signs following. Then you can say to them, 'Good, you are safe on this. You do not need lessons on this any more. We can go on from here.'

"This is not true of most students, however. They have to have a review from time to time especially on the principles contained in this letter. They will not like these lessons as well as the lessons about sitting on cloud nine, inner initiations, and seeing visions. But as important as those lessons are, they are of no use at all without these basic principles because they are what make truth demonstrable.

"Many metaphysical teachings today and many students are going backward instead of forward because they are all so eager to sit around and talk about this lovely God that they will not come right down to brass tacks and say, 'Yes, God is lovely, but He is not doing anything for this world—only for those who make themselves consciously one with truth.' Most students do not want to do that hard work, but as a teacher, you will have to decide whether you want numbers or whether you want to attract only those who do really want to get somewhere in consciousness.

"You who have had a background of years and years of study may now be just assimilating what is contained in this letter, tying a string around it, and realizing, 'Oh, I have known all these things he has been saying for years, but I did not tie them all together in one bundle, nor perhaps see the full significance of them as I do now.'

"The value comes only when you stop reading and sit in meditation, 'Ah, Father, I know now all the truth, but how about an extra word from You?' That is the Word that brings the signs following. The roof could cave in, and the omnipresence of God would not stop it; but a meditation with signs following would stop the roof from falling in. It would hang suspended without touching you—not by your power, not by your goodness, not by your love: by God's grace. You can be sure that God's grace is on the field only when that assurance is there.

"No matter how much a teacher teaches his students, he should not let them go away until there has been a meditation to consolidate the lesson, so that the students can assimilate it and the seal be put on it. No human teacher can do that. God places the seal on the lesson when the meditation takes place. In the concluding meditation you need no words or thoughts. You are sitting in a state of receptivity to let God place the seal on the lesson and the meditation. That is when you bring it all into livingness; you bring it down from the head to the heart."

Joel S. Goldsmith, *1963 Instructions for Teaching the Infinite Way.*

Publisher's Note: Chapters 3, 4, 5, 6, 8 and 10 introduce a special section on teaching the Infinite Way, taken from the recordings of Joel S. Goldsmith.

*Chapter Four*

# The Parenthesis

Throughout the writings it is pointed out that our function is not to improve humanhood: it is not to find an ideal companion for a person, an ideal home, or to make his body physically well. The Infinite Way has nothing to do with changing human conditions. The function of God is not to mend broken bones, to go out and get more dollars or automobiles, or to annihilate our enemies. As a matter of fact, whatever the nature or function of God is, already is. Our function is to leave "this world" because we have discovered that there is a "My kingdom" and "My kingdom" is not of "this world."[1] That immediately sets up a whole new world for an individual.

How do we leave this world? How do we stop taking thought for this world? The question is not how, but that it must be done. How it is done is an individual experience. I can tell about my own way of arriving at whatever stage of that process I have reached, but I cannot be sure that that is the way that will lead others to it. Beyond all question of doubt, as long as we are taking thought for what we eat, what we drink, or wherewithal we are clothed, we are not following the message of the Infinite Way.

Such an idea pulls the foundation out from many students. It leaves them with nothing on which to stand, and that is the intent. "He hangeth the earth on nothing."[2] If we have a single thought in our mind, we are going to cling to that thought. Any concept of God, any concept of what we expect of God, any concept of the fruitage we are looking for stands in the way of God's demonstration, because that is not opening oneself to the way or the will of God.

## Discovering God's Will

Ever since we were born, we have been thwarting the will of God, doing everything our parents, teachers, or society told us, everything that good manners told us to do. How often have we turned to God and asked, "God, don't You have something to say about how my life should be lived? After all, You authored my life. Have You nothing to say about its mode or manner of living?" If we did that, then even if our parents wanted us to be a bookkeeper or something else, eventually we would be what God intended us to be; or instead of having our wish of the moment fulfilled we might find that God's will is something entirely different for us. But we will never know God's will while we are holding a thought or a concept in our mind when we go to God.

Too many letters that come to me read something like this, "Thank you for this healing. Now I can go back and take care of my grandchildren," or "Now I can go back and look for a job," without a single thought that this miracle of Grace might have some further meaning. But the mind was on one thing only: attaining health, supply, companionship, or whatever the object.

Our function is not to improve humanhood, and yet, judging from what students say when they ask for help, are not most of them trying to change human conditions? Students could read Infinite Way writings for ten years and never discover that idea in them unless they themselves were already volleying back and forth between human good today and human lack tomorrow.

The teacher's function is not to change human conditions. No, it is the function of the teacher to impart the truth to the student so that when he sits down to pray or to meditate, he goes to God completely pure. No student should outline in his thought what he wants God to do, what result he wants, what fruitage. To do that is to stand in God's way and in his own way of receiving God.

When we pray, we must have no concept in our mind at all as to what we desire. Even if we ourselves appear to be sick or to have a sick or a blind patient, we have no right to want the opposite. We must be anchored in *isness:* the eternal perfection and harmony of Being.

### *Improved Humanhood Is Not the Goal of the Spiritual Path*

Our only desire should be for Christ-realization, that the spirit of the Lord may be upon us and through us produce Its mighty works. What mighty works? We do not know. We only know that in some measure Christ-realization will appear as improved health, improved supply, improved companionship, but that is not the fruitage of our work: those are the added things. The fruitage of our work is the realization of the transcendental presence and power, the awareness that we live, not by might, but by Grace. "I live; yet not I, but Christ liveth in me"[3] is not a prayer *for* something. It is a statement of what happens after prayer; it is the fruitage of prayer that we do not have to take thought for our life, because the Christ is now living our life.

After students have been on the spiritual path they sometimes seem to have a feeling of frustration and let-down because they had expected to be wafted up to cloud nine. They do not realize that this work sets up a battle between the spirit and the flesh. Even while they are looking for the body to get well, the

Spirit is trying to tell them, "I do not want you to have bodily health; I want you to have *Me*. I do not want you to companion with people: I want you to companion with *Me*." It shocks them because companioning with the Christ is not what they had expected or wanted.

The very fact that students have a want is really the battle between the spirit and the flesh. Students are unable to find this out for themselves, because in coming to this work, their whole intent is usually on improving humanhood. Here and there one may deny this, but I have not yet found it to be true of most students, although I have found a few such individuals. They have been only a few out of all the world, and the fruitage in their lives is entirely different from that in the lives of the others.

The others find their improved humanhood to some degree and get stuck there; the few keep going on, and on, and on, and eventually forget whether their humanhood is good today or bad today, because they are not concentrating on that. The degree of evolved spiritual consciousness attained this year is the degree of harmony experienced next year and the year after.

## *What Is the Parenthesis?*

The period from conception to the grave is a parenthesis in eternity which can best be illustrated with a ring. One parenthesis might cover a quarter or less of the ring, another parenthesis another quarter, and a third parenthesis still another one. If we think of the second parenthesis as where we are now in time, then unless there was a parenthesis prior to the present one, we have no basis for believing that when we leave this present parenthesis we will enter another one. The point is that if there were no parenthesis before, why should we think there will be one afterwards? In other words, if we began, why do we not end? Only on the premise that there was a parenthesis before our present one can we understand what is happening to us in this life.

## *What Will Our Situation Be in the Next Parenthesis?*

And what is going to happen to us in the next parenthesis? Will we be born and live in a slave-country or in a poverty-stricken country, if there are any such countries left on earth? What is the possibility of our being born into adverse circumstances?

Whatever treasures we lay up in this parenthesis we will carry into the next parenthesis. And what are those treasures? Certainly we cannot carry with us any measure of wealth or property we have acquired, no matter how great it may be. We cannot carry this physical sense of body with us either, or any member of our family, no matter how dear to us. No, we go into the next experience alone. All we can carry with us is what has been stored up in our consciousness. So, if we have laid up flesh, lust, ambition, greed, selfishness, that is what we must carry with us into our next parenthesis.

In Oriental teaching this principle is known as karma. Christians call it the law of as-ye-sow-so-shall-ye-reap, and they are warned that any sowing a person does while here on earth is carried over into the next life and will greet him in his next parenthesis.

As students, then, it behooves us to give all the time and effort we can to our study, to our meditation, and to the practice of spiritual principles, so that when we leave here, whenever that may be, at least we will carry with us a foundation for the new experience. This helps explain some of the good and some of the evil that have happened to us in this parenthesis.

## *We Are Responsible for Our Life*

Are we not carrying with us here some of what we laid up to bring across from a former parenthesis, whether it was the fleshly mind or the spirit? Some people believe that we suffer for the sins of our parents, or that we benefit from their prowess. In other words, there is a belief that heredity is responsible for the good that comes to us or the evil that befalls us. This I do not accept.

Even if we are born into wealth, it is not because of our parents. It is because of our consciousness. If we have healthy parents and enjoy health, we did not inherit their health: we brought our health with us. There are many healthy parents who have sick children; there are many sick parents who have healthy children. So, the ancient Hebrews were right when they taught that each one makes his own life and must take the responsibility for it. God is not "visiting the iniquity of the fathers upon the children unto the third or fourth generation."[4] No, each individual brings to his life his own stored-up consciousness.

We are responsible for our life—not our parents and not our surroundings. If there is not a developed consciousness in us, we will be a victim of our own nothingness. If peace, love, joy, and fulfillment are in our consciousness, nothing in this world can keep us from that kind of an experience. We are the product of what is within us, and if we glimpse that, we can then go on and develop or continue to develop that spiritual consciousness which externalizes as a fulfilled life. If in our ignorance we do not glimpse it, we will just live out or whole lifespan bemoaning our fate and blaming someone else for it.

### Recognize and Draw upon the Infinite Resources of Spirit

We do have infinite capacity, because God is really the Self of us. Through meditation, and only through meditation, can we make immediate contact and become consciously at-one with our source, thereby drawing upon Its infinity. Once we learn to draw upon our Source, there is no handicap in our experience that cannot be overcome. There must be that desire, otherwise it cannot be.

For example, Alcoholics Anonymous has blessed many persons, but there are others who have tried it who have not benefitted from it because that inner drive to overcome alcoholism was not there. There are any number of students in the Infinite Way who have no greater desire than to be healed or to try to get up on a platform to display their ego.

If teachers can impart to students the idea that there is no limit to their spiritual capacity, even to attaining full Christhood, those in whom that spark is awakened will go on from there and put forth every effort possible in order to attain the goal, realizing that whatever degree of Christ-consciousness is stored up here is the degree that will be carried into the next incarnation or parenthesis. Even if they do not return to earth again, they are still incarnating as living beings wherever or whatever the circumstance. We may call it a parenthesis, however, because while it may be lived here or it may not be lived here, it is still a segment of one's total experience.

### Emerging from the
### Parenthesis into Eternity

Through an understanding of this, parents develop a greater sense of responsibility toward their children, because they realize that in imparting spiritual wisdom to the child, they are giving him a far greater treasure than the dollars they might leave him, or even the education they plan to provide.

We go from parenthesis to parenthesis, until through higher and higher spiritual attainment, the parenthesis becomes weaker and weaker. Finally it fades out. Then we are no longer living in the parenthesis: we are living in eternity, and yet each one is maintaining unto the end of time his individuality. Living in eternity does not mean an absorption into Deity.

Each one of us has an individual mode and form of expression. There will never come a time when we will be without it.

We were created with it, and it is our permanent identity. We may be a male in one incarnation and a female in another, depending on what our purpose is in incarnating. But it will always be *I*. Always *I*, in its individual identity, will be looking out, and whether the form appears as a male or a female form, or whatever form it takes, *I* will always be *I*. When you and I were formed in the bosom of the Father in the beginning, each form was as an individual expression of that Infinity.

Only through understanding the nature of every life-experience as a parenthesis in eternity does life have meaning. That explains why I am in the work of the Infinite Way. My life-experience did not come about accidentally or by claiming that I was favored of God. It showed me that I must be a progressively unfolding state of consciousness, and that somehow or other I must have been on this path and evolved toward this point.

On no other basis than the on-goingness and continuity of life can we account for what is happening to us and to the people of the world. As we see some persons walk through life without becoming victims of its injustices and inequalities and then see others who are forever plagued by misfortune, we know there must be something within them that seems to have determined their life-experience. Especially is this evident in some who have been reared in the very finest of families and given the best of culture and education and yet who turn out to be the "black sheep" of the family. The experience of such persons is actually their attained state of consciousness.

It is important for a student to understand this subject because while he cannot go back and live each life over again or overcome the handicaps of his past parenthesis, he can begin over again now. It is foolish for a person of any age not to be willing to look squarely in the face the truth that someday he will be marching on to another experience. If a person is only in his teens now, he should face the fact that the day is coming when he will give place to another generation and will march on to another experience. The treasures he lays up for himself of a spiritual, cultural, or educational nature comprise the enlightenment he will carry with him into the next parenthesis.

For most persons such an idea will be of no interest. Their attitude will be that they will take care of that when the time comes. There will, however, be the remnant of those ready to hear this truth who respond to it and do something about it.

## Across the Desk

In *The Altitude of Prayer*[10] there is a beautiful chapter on life called, "This is Immortality," which further emphasizes the nature of this life as a parenthesis:

Life, real life, is lived in consciousness; it is lived in the secret place within ourselves. We do not begin to suspect what the God-life can be until we have contacted that fountain of Life within us. We are not really living if we think of life as something that exists between what is called birth and death. That is not life.

This life is, as one of the ancient mystics called it, a parenthesis in eternity. It is often pictured as a circle and is usually spoken of as being eternal. But if we live only inside the parenthesis that begins with birth and ends at death, we are missing the greatest part of life, the eternal, infinite, and immortal structure in which we discover God's creation. In this brief interval called the parenthesis, we live largely in man's creation, and we miss God's creation. We miss the life and love of God; we miss sharing in the life and love of one another.

If we know each other only as human beings, we are cheating ourselves of a tremendous delight. We are of spring of God, filled with the love, the life, and the spirit of God, and this we must recognize. All the joys of spiritual being are embodied in us for sharing. That is why we are on earth.

Someday you will have an experience and learn that you are I, that your Self cannot be confined in time or in space, but that you exist beyond time and beyond space. Then you will know the secret of preexistence. You will know that 'before Abraham was, I am,' and I will be with you unto the end of the world, whether I, Joel, say that, or whether I, you, say it, for there is only one I on this earth. That I is the identity of those who have gone out of our physical sight; It is our identity; and It is the identity of those still unborn.

And this is immortality.

This brief excerpt is just one example of the rich spiritual treasures found in this magnificent book by Joel. Reading and studying it will reveal to you a whole new dimension of life.

TEACHING THE INFINITE WAY
"Only Consciousness Can Impart Spiritual Principles"

"In teaching the Infinite Way, the teacher is imparting his own consciousness, and if he does not know what he is trying to teach, he cannot impart it. He cannot teach what is not his own consciousness, even though he may be able to recite pages of quotations from the books.

"For example, a teacher must keep in mind constantly—so that it becomes a part of his very being—the truth that God is not a power over anything, that he is not trying to use God as a power or to use truth over error, but rather he is to live out from and impart the consciousness that there is no other power, presence, or law because God is omnipotent. This must become as much a part of the teacher's being as the A B C's.

"In addition to this, two other points separate the message

of the Infinite Way from all other spiritual messages. The first of these is the nature of error as universal and impersonal. In our work we are never dealing with an erroneous person whom we are going to make right or a disease for which we are going to substitute health. We are not attempting to correct, reform, or heal a person. We recognize that all error has its basis in a universal belief in two powers, and therefore our treatment is never aimed at a person.

"Above all, we do not use psychological approaches such as, 'If you were just grateful, you would get healed'; or 'If you read twelve pages of the books every day, you would get healed'; or 'If you would just be more loving to your husband'; or 'If you would be more patient with your wife'. Those psychological approaches have nothing whatsoever to do with our work.

"Our work is a continuous abiding in the truth that all evil has its basis in the carnal mind, that is, in a universal belief in two powers. Therefore, we are constantly impersonalizing. If we are not living that life of impersonalization, there is no use trying to teach it because even if we use the right words in teaching, we are not imparting it to the consciousness of the students. They are not receiving the teaching because of the words we say, but because of the consciousness to which we are able to elevate them.

"The first responsibility of an individual is not to attempt to heal or to try to teach, but to work to develop within himself the consciousness of these major principles, so that when he does go out to heal or teach he has the necessary uplifted spiritual consciousness with which to work."

Teaching Spiritual Principles

"Infinite Way principles must be uppermost in the teacher's mind. Whether it is an individual coming to the teacher for healing or spiritual guidance or whether there are three, five, or ten students coming together once a week for some instruction, a teacher cannot give it to them, even if he takes the books and works from them, unless he has a clear-cut awareness of the specific principles which must constantly be brought to light so as to change individual consciousness.

"If a teacher were to spend a whole hour with one person or a little group, bringing out the point of not attempting to change bad humanhood into good humanhood, but rather learning to ignore the appearance, go down the middle path, and abide in spiritual reality, when they left the teacher that day, that principle would be impressed on them. It will not remain, however, and that is why the same lesson must be repeated over, and over, and over again, and one by one, each one will say— sometimes this month, and sometimes five years from now— 'Oh, you know what I have discovered? You do not try to change humanhood!'

"So a teacher should never be surprised when a student tells him that he has had a revelation such as that evil is not personal. When truth is revealed to a person, even though he has read about it many times, it is an original discovery to him because it is something that never registered with him before. Intellectually he may have known it but not inwardly. A teacher or practitioner will not succeed in giving one person or a group a treatment or a lesson unless he has in mind some specific point, because it is that specific point that raises the consciousness of the patient or the student and gives him a working principle."

### Teaching the Three O's

"In teaching the meaning of omniscience, omnipotence, and omnipresence, not only must the teacher spend an hour explaining to the student the meaning of each of those three words, but he has to give another lesson on the same subject a month from then, because even if a student remembers the lesson, he probably has not yet attained the consciousness of it. Simply giving those three words to a student will do exactly nothing for him. One has to spend a long, long time with each one of those words, showing specifically its meaning and its application.

"In order to teach more about prayer, the teacher might say to the students, 'Do you know what omniscience means? If not, let us refer to a dictionary, and understand that omniscience means all-knowing: God, the all-knowing; God, the all-wise. Now pause for a moment and think: God is the all-knowing, God is the all-wise. What would you like to tell God in a treatment or a prayer?'

"By that concrete, specific example, the teacher closes the students' mouths and their minds. They almost have to laugh at themselves. 'Just think of little old me trying to tell God what I need, when God is omniscient. Think of my trying to tell God when I need it, when God knows the very moment every blossom should bloom and when every fruit tree should bear fruit.' Nothing except a concrete example like that will stop the mind of the person who has erroneously been taught to pray or treat in a certain way.

"Omnipotence—all-power? What would you like God to do? To what would you like It to do it? To whom would you like It to do it? God is all-power, meaning the only power, so is there anything on which to use God-power? But if the teacher or the practitioner is not fully aware of the meaning and application of these two words, how can he teach them or convey the consciousness of those words to anyone? No student can gather any more from a practitioner or teacher than the practitioner's or teacher's consciousness—no more!

"It is hopeless for a practitioner or a teacher to expect to have a great influence on students if he, himself, is still living in the consciousness of wanting a God-power to do something or is trying to meet the problem on the level of the problem.

"To be God-governed, we must have surrendered our own life to the point where we are less and less dependent on human footsteps, less and less trying to turn the bad into the good, and more and more abiding in the realization of God's grace. Less and less are we fighting evil, less and less are we seeking a power with which to overcome evil; less and less are we seeking to have our enemies destroyed.

"Instead we are living out from a consciousness which is more and more ignoring the appearances and abiding in the realization that God's grace is the sufficiency unto this universe and is our sufficiency. God's grace is our sufficiency, and whatever is to be accomplished in our life must be accomplished by God's grace, not by fighting an enemy.

"At this stage of our work it is better not to struggle against temptation because even if the evil condition persists for a while, we are refraining from taking up the sword, and we are relying on the truth of its nonpower. Better than fighting and resisting the discord and making it a power, even if it appears to persist while we are holding it in its nothingness, is to acknowledge, 'You are no part of me, and I want no part of you. You are not of God, and therefore you can be only an appearance, a temptation, an illusion.'

"Since in reality evil is not a power, it is far better to 'suffer it to be so now'[5] than to sit up all night fighting it, battling it, and making a reality of it."

### Bringing the Christ-Activity to the Situation

"These principles must have become so embodied in our own consciousness that it is automatic to ignore the person who says, 'I have a terrible pain. Will you do something about it?' or where it has become automatic to disregard the degree of the fever or the size of the lump, and come right down to the middle path of ignoring the appearance and abiding in spiritual reality until that place of stillness is reached where we can let the power of God be made evident through the still, small voice.

"We must train ourselves to walk down the street realizing, 'Not bad humanhood, not good humanhood: Christhood!' We must have blinkers on our eyes, so that we do not see what is on the left or on the right, but see right down the middle: Christhood! We acknowledge Christhood in the midst of us, Christhood as true individual being, the being of human, animal, vegetable, mineral.

"'I am come that they might have life, and that they might have it more abundantly.'[6] That does not mean that we of ourselves have the power to do anything in the healing work. We have to keep knowing that *I*, the Christ, am come, and then let the Christ do Its work.

"Neither you nor I, nor the whole Infinite Way, can change the history of this world. Only the Christ can do that, and our function is to bring the Christ into activity. Once students catch the idea that the Christ is the liberator, we have done all we can for them. After that, they do not need us. Our function is to set them free and to know that the Christ is the activity of their consciousness. The Christ is the bread, the meat, the wine, the water; the Christ is the resurrection. In proportion as we know this, we yield ourselves to the Christ and let It raise us up.

"It was the Christ that raised up Jesus from the tomb. 'He that raised up Christ from the dead shall also quicken your mortal bodies by his Spirit that dwelleth in you.'[7] That spirit is the Christ, the son of God, and that son of God will raise up this whole earth. You will not; I will not; the Christ, the spirit of God in man, will; but we have to bring that Christ to conscious remembrance."

## The Continuity of Revelation

"Every individual has access to infinity because God constitutes individual consciousness. Every individual can know anything and everything he desires to know. Scripture confirms this truth: 'And they shall all be taught of God.'[8] But if we are going around looking for a God, we will not be taught of God. That teaching comes only when we come into the awareness that God constitutes our individual consciousness, and therefore our individual consciousness is the source of infinite wisdom and eternal harmony. What further will be revealed to you or me, nobody can tell, but because God is infinite, we may be assured that there is more to be revealed than ever has been revealed.

"Let no one ever convince us that the end of revelation has come. One of the disastrous things in the world is to believe that all the truth is in the Old Testament and the New Testament, as if there were no truth before the Old Testament, and as if God closed up shop after the New Testament. If God is the revelator of truth, then before Abraham was, God was revealing truth. And since 'I am with you alway, even unto the end of the world,'[9] God will be revealing truth to individuals unto the end of the world.

"One of our prime functions as teachers or practitioners is to lead those who come to us to where they draw forth their health and supply from within their own being. We must explain to them that at the present time we are the bridge over which they travel, but that if we do not go away, the Comforter will not come to them and that they, in their turn, must carry on this work. If we became the best healers in the world, we would have the whole world to heal, which we could not do, unless we could teach others, and unless others could take up this work."

Joel S. Goldsmith, *1963 Instructions for Teaching the Infinite Way.*

*Chapter Five*

# Infinite Way Pearls

Several major contributions have been made to the world through the Infinite Way. One of these does away with belief, faith, and hope in God as a word in the mind or as existing some place remote from us, and reveals instead that the illumined consciousness of an individual is God. When a person has the mind that was in Christ Jesus, he has the God-mind. When he does not have the mind that was in Christ Jesus, in reality he has no God, for there is no God separate and apart from the illumined consciousness of an individual. The unillumined consciousness is not God, but the illumined consciousness is.

Is there any principle in the Infinite Way greater than the truth that God is individual consciousness, your consciousness and mine? This is the top secret because to my knowledge it is the first time it has been revealed. Everyone has a consciousness; therefore, everyone has God; but there are two states of consciousness: the illumined consciousness and the unillumined consciousness. Your consciousness and mine are either unillumined or illumined. It may not be wholly unillumined and it may not be wholly illumined, but it is at some stage in between.

If the unillumined have a God at all, it is a God separate and

apart from their own being. It may be something as paganistic
as a man on a cross or a man who walked the streets of Galilee.
But if a person has a man for a God, either the man of Galilee
or an old gentleman up in the sky with a great big book, mark-
ing down a person's good days and his bad days, he is totally
unillumined. The closer a person comes to the realization that
the kingdom of God is within him, the more quickly he will go
from the unillumined to the illumined, until he finally reaches
the realization:

> God constitutes my individual consciousness;
> therefore, my consciousness is imbued with
> the quantities and qualities of God—
> not just a little bit but the fullness of God.

The highest illumination involves an awareness of our true
identity, and as we come to the realization that God constitutes
our consciousness, the closer we come to illumination and the
more we can relax.

### The Omnipresence of Consciousness

To know the nature of Consciousness as omniscience is a
step toward still further illumination. You become a state of
complete awareness, a state of listening, and you can rest with
nothing to tell God.

The closer you come to a realization of your consciousness
as omnipotence, the less you fear other powers. You rest in
peace for the remainder of your days, because if your consciousness is omnipotence you will not fear what mortal man
can do to you. You have put off mortality and have been
clothed with immortality.

Furthermore, when you realize that God is your consciousness, that is a realization of omnipresence because your con-

sciousness is not separate and apart from you. Even if you mount up to heaven, your consciousness is with you, or you will not be conscious that you are in heaven; and if you go to hell, unless your consciousness is with you, you will not even know you are in hell. So whither can you flee from your consciousness?

When you know that your consciousness is not constituted of your education, your parents' reputation, or your wealth, but of the activities, the quantities, and the qualities of God, you can walk up and down the world with or without purse and scrip because you are carrying your invisible checkbook on Infinity.

### Nothing Can Be Added
### to Infinite Consciousness

A child entering his first day of school already has all the knowledge that he will have when his college degree is conferred upon him. He has it in consciousness, and what the teacher does is to draw it out of his consciousness, thereby making it available at this level of his life. Every individual has all the truth in his consciousness that he will have when he is fully Christed. No one can add to his consciousness of truth. He already has it. The teacher is drawing it forth from the student's consciousness to the level of conscious awareness. What is real is in God-consciousness, and if it is in God-consciousness, it is in individual consciousness. Students must become consciously aware of the truth that since God is their consciousness, they already possess infinity and can close their eyes, turn within, and draw it forth. The kingdom of God is within you, so if you want anything, go within.

For seventeen hundred years, much religion has separated man from God and has convinced him that the way to get his good is not to go to God, but to conform to a ceremony, a rite, or a ritual: make a contribution, light a candle, say a prayer. The kingdom of God is not out there in a form: it is within you. It is your very consciousness.

## God As Individual Consciousness

Once we know that God constitutes individual consciousness, then God is the consciousness of the individual, and the illumined consciousness of that individual is his God. How much
God does he have? As much as he can accept and become aware
of. He can have a little bit of God or a great deal of God, and
eventually he can have the whole of the mind that was in Christ
Jesus if he continues developing and evolving to that point.

Always we come back to the truth that anything we can
think about God cannot possibly be God, because that thought
is only an idea in our mind, and an idea or a concept in the
mind cannot be God. Whatever is in our mind is an effect, and
the thinker is the cause of that effect. Therefore, if there is a
God, it is not the human thinker, but the illumined mind of the
individual. Attainment does not lie in finding a God: attainment lies in developing our individual consciousness to its
Christhood, or at least to some degree thereof.

It is true that no individual can undertake the attaining of
the mind of Christ Jesus unless the grace of God has been
bestowed upon him because without the grace of God he would
have no interest in it. The things of the Spirit are foolishness
with man, so there is little use to try to develop spiritually the
person who does not within himself hunger and thirst after the
spiritual life and give some indication of the degree of his hungering and thirsting and his appreciation and understanding of
what it is he is seeking.

There is a difference between the person who is merely trying to attain health and the person seeking illumination. A person whose primary concern is to be healed by God is merely saying, "I cannot be healed medically, so I am willing to be healed
spiritually, and I don't think it makes any difference whether I
am healed materially or spiritually, except that being healed
spiritually is easier." What I think such a person means is that it

is less expensive. But it does make a difference. There is no God to heal a person now any more than there was a God to heal him yesterday or the day before yesterday. If there is a God to heal a person tomorrow, there must have been a God to heal him yesterday. And where was It? What is not generally understood is that the healing agency is the illumined consciousness of an individual, and the difference in the measure of healing lies not in God, but in the degree of illumination of the individual.

### What Is Illumination?

The second major contribution of the Infinite Way to the world is to understand what illumination consists of, what we mean by illumination or the illumined consciousness, and how to attain it.

An illumined consciousness is the state of consciousness that does not hate, fear, or love error in any form. That is illumination: that is Christ-consciousness or spiritual consciousness. When consciousness is awakened to the realization that since God is "of purer eyes than to behold evil, and canst not look on iniquity,"[1] then individual consciousness must be lifted to that place where it, too, is too pure to behold iniquity, and it does not have evil to overcome, rise above, or destroy.

Illumined consciousness is always at rest in the realization that there is a *My* kingdom and that this is *My* kingdom. The world is only "this world"[2] when we are accepting two powers. It is not a second world: it is an imaginary world held in our minds, and in the degree that we have only one power, one presence, one cause, one effect, one reality, are we illumined, and in that degree is this world overcome.

We are of this world when we judge by appearances. We are the unillumined when we see sin, disease, death, lack, and limitation as something to be overcome, as power. We are the illumined consciousness when we have perceived inwardly that all appearances are illusory: they are not forms, conditions, or persons. They are states of illusion. When this is recognized we can be obedient to the Master's revelation, "Resist not evil.[3]. . . Put up again thy sword."[4] We are not illumined when we take up the physical sword or the mental sword, or when we feel we have to protect ourselves from the evils of this world.

Once we have perceived that individual illumined consciousness is Christhood, we have nothing further to do, Christhood does it all. We teach students that the nature of God is omniscience, and that is why we do not have to tell It anything; God is omnipotence, and because God is the only power there is no evil. As we reach the stage of illumined consciousness, we must know that the God we are talking about is omnipresent as individual consciousness. It is that *My*-consciousness, God-consciousness.

> In God-consciousness,
> there is nothing to be influenced or used.
> God-consciousness is Itself omniscient
> and knows my need. Because God is my individual
> consciousness, all that God is, my consciousness is.

Every Infinite Way book reveals this truth, but a person cannot understand it until at a certain point in his evolutionary experience it hits him and he says, "Whereas I was blind, now I see."[5] From then on, he begins to relax.

### Consciousness Is a Law of Resurrection

"Resurrection, in its mystical sense, means resurrecting the son of God out of the tomb of the physical senses."[6]

We are born into a physical sense of life, thinking with and through the human mind alone. Resurrection means lifting up the son of God in us until the son of God, not the physical senses or the human mind, replaces our mind with that mind that was in Christ Jesus. It is also resurrection in the sense of rising out of the physical sense of body. But when the son of God is raised up in us, and we gain the realization of spiritual consciousness as governing all form, then we have a more spiritual sense of body and the universe. Where have we left God? Spiritual consciousness becomes God in action: your spiritual consciousness, my spiritual consciousness, the spiritual consciousness of any individual who has attained it.

The revelation of life lived by Grace instead of under the law consists of the revelation of the consciousness of the individual as a law of resurrection, healing, and protection to the body, business, home, and well-being in every form, and we begin to see how consciousness—the consciousness of the individual— even without taking thought and without being directed, becomes the law of harmony unto our experience.[7]

In this brief passage is the whole secret.

### *Consciousness Draws unto Itself Its Own*

Let us assume that in 1946 Joel was the only person who had caught these two principles under the name of the Infinite Way, and in 1947 they were presented to the public in a book. The human way of introducing such a book to the world would be to get a publisher, advertise, give lectures, and invite the press to hear and report on them, and to send out free copies to ministers, thereby projecting these ideas into the human mind. That might bring opposition, and there could be persecution, but in time consciousness would begin to absorb it.

There is a way, however, that was taught to me, which has nothing to do with such promotional methods. That way was to sit in my home and wait for somebody to come to me. Eventually three people came to me by automobile from Ohio to California of their own will and accord. Four married couples in California later came, followed by others. After that came invitations to speak in metaphysical centers. All came; none was sought! I steadfastly obeyed my orders to stay in my home.

A metaphysical teacher sent a copy of *The Infinite Way* to Henry Thomas Hamblin in England which led him to publish an article he wrote called "The Infinite Way." The response was so great and the demand for the book so big that George Allen and Unwin of London asked to publish it. Finally major American publishers asked to publish my writings. So a pathway was beaten to my door without a human act.

Behind this is the principle that if God poured this message into my consciousness, it could not have been to make me healthy, wealthy, and wise. God could not have been considering doing me a favor. It was really not being poured into my consciousness as an individual: it was being poured into human consciousness, and I was sufficiently attuned and prepared to receive it. But if God was pouring this into human consciousness, then God must also be preparing the consciousness of others to receive it. So God, in His mysterious way, and it is a mysterious way, brought all of these things about that have now established the Infinite Way on a world-wide basis.

### God-Consciousness Expresses As Individual Consciousness

The consciousness which is God is nothing while It is floating around in the air; it is only when the consciousness which is God is realized as the consciousness of an individual that It functions on his level of life. Therefore, as truth becomes my consciousness, and I abide in It, It touches students somewhere and they are drawn to It. Humanly I could not do that.

We have no way of knowing how God acts, but I do know

the way by which It acts. There is only one Consciousness, and, as individuals lift themselves, they reach the consciousness that can bless them and which they can bless. It has to be a two-way street, otherwise it cannot operate. By Grace, this vision has been given to the world.

All those in need must eventually find God. God will appear to them as the right teacher or practitioner when that need exists, but they can find God appearing as books—Infinite Way books—or they can find God as teachers, because those who are seeking God are the same consciousness as those who have found It. So whether they find It as Joel's books or find It as an Infinite Way teacher, they are finding that which they sought: God-awareness.

## *Omnipresent Consciousness*
## *As Omniscience and Omnipotence*

Our "pearl of great price"[8] is the awareness that God constitutes individual consciousness, my consciousness, your consciousness, and the consciousness of everyone in the world—not that everyone is aware of God as his consciousness, but that is the truth to which he eventually must be awakened. The end of the search for God comes when a person discovers that God constitutes his consciousness and that God is not to be found in holy mountains or holy temples, in Jerusalem, Rome, or Boston. God is to be found only as individual consciousness, yours and mine. That is our great pearl. In proportion as we become aware of God as our consciousness are we illumined.

Our great pearl has another facet, too, and that is that the illumination, which reveals God as our individual consciousness, also reveals that the nature of that consciousness is omniscience, omnipotence, omnipresence. I do not have to pray to my consciousness in the sense of telling it anything, trying to influence it, or trying to buy its favors. I have to relax in it, because God's thoughts are not my thoughts. There is no way that my thoughts can influence God.

To accept my consciousness as omniscience means that I must sit in the silence and let my consciousness speak to me through the still, small voice, or the thundering voice that makes the earth melt. But the point is that I am illumined in proportion as I know that I do not have to seek outside myself. I do not need to tell God, importune, beg, plead, praise, bribe, or try to influence God or tithe with God. God is omniscience, and my contact with God is to remain in the attitude of listening.

Furthermore, the pearl that God is individual consciousness consists of the fact that God is omnipotence and therefore I need no God-power. I am not seeking God, because there is nothing for God to overcome. What I am doing is becoming a state of receptivity so that the voice can utter Itself through me. Not by praying to God to do away with wars and tyrants, but by letting our divine consciousness manifest Itself in silence through the still, small voice, will peace on earth be established individually and collectively. We do not tell God where to go, what country to go to, what tyrant or politician to handle; we do not tell God of the evils of this world and then ask Him to do something about them: we abide in stillness.

Since God is omnipresence, It has no powers to overcome or destroy. It merely has to be allowed an inlet and an outlet to this universe, and then the evils of this world are dissolved, because they do not exist as powers or realities. They exist only as mirage, illusion, or illusory concepts produced by the belief in two powers.

Again, our pearl consists of the awareness that God omnipresent as my very consciousness, so that the place whereon I stand is always holy ground. If I go up to heaven, it is holy ground; if I make my bed in hell, it is holy ground; if I walk through "the valley of the shadow of death,"[9] it is holy ground, because my consciousness and God-consciousness are one. God constitutes my very consciousness even in the midst of sin, disease, death, lack, or limitation, and my awareness of this dissolves the pictures of sense, and the erroneous appearances to which we have reacted. Now we no longer react to appearances. Rather, because of their illusory nature, we understand their non-power.

## The "Pearl" of Spiritual Power

Eventually we come to the greatest revelation, the very top revelation, that has been given to the world by the Infinite Way, and that is the nature of spiritual power. Spiritual power cannot be used by man; it cannot be influenced by man; it cannot be controlled by man; it cannot be made to do something by or for man. Spiritual power operates through the still, small voice to govern man.

As we individually open our consciousness to the Christ-government, It governs us individually, and yet It does not limit Itself to governing us alone. Every time It comes to us, It is also released into human consciousness so that even in one generation It can change many facets of the consciousness of mankind. It is that which is permeating the earth today. It does not mean that four billion people will have to awaken individually to the Christ; it means that because "ten"[10] righteous men are admitting the Christ into human consciousness , eventually there will be no human consciousness left. As new generations are born, they will be born into a higher consciousness, which is now being established on earth. It will not be necessary for them to go through the experiences of their parents or to make the same mistakes.

Many persons have known that if only they could lay hold of spiritual power, they could overcome the problems and troubles of the world, but the error in their attitude has been that they have always sought a spiritual power that could be used. There is no such thing; there is no spiritual power that can be used. There is a spiritual power to which we can submit ourselves, and that is the power of our consciousness when our consciousness no longer fears, hates, or loves error in any form.

### Impersonalization, Essential to Illumination

The greatest problem that comes to me with patients and students is that they do not understand the 1959 work.[11] Somehow the problem that is brought up is always a person, a condition, or a series of events, and very few seem able to grasp the fact that we are not dealing with persons, but dealing with appearances which we understand to be of the nature of illusion.

Since it takes years and years before students and patients can realize that we are dealing not with persons or conditions but with universal beliefs, it is the practitioner or teacher who must be so evolved that no matter who comes or what, there is the recognition, "This is not a person or a condition I am meeting. This is a universal hypnotism or anti-Christ." In the recognition of that, a person should be done with it.

No one is evolved spiritually who is still trying to reform or heal people, or remove sins or diseases. No one has attained illumination who does not have such an evolved consciousness that he refuses to take a person into his treatment, prayer, or meditation and recognizes, "Wait a minute, I have nothing to do with thee. Get thee behind me, Satan. I am dealing only with a temptation to accept appearances."

The major responsibility is on the practitioner or teacher. That does not mean that he can guarantee that every patient is going to be healed or taught. The patient or student may have a wall up that refuses to let in spiritual light by insisting that the problem is a person or a condition. Eventually he must yield or he will not be able to make it. I have many patients with whom I have been working for as long as twelve years who do not catch this principle and do not get their healing. They are holding that wall up that insists that this is a person, either the "me" of themselves or of the other person. In such a situation the practitioner may not be able to break through.

In most cases and with most persons, sooner or later there is a yielding, but we are not illumined except in the proportion that we have impersonalized and are no longer blaming persons for their troubles, regardless of what they may be. While we are waiting for them to awaken, we must say to ourselves, "At least I am awake. I am not holding you in bondage. This is not a person; this is universal hypnotism." Then we drop it, because the minute we begin to work against universal hypnotism we have taken up the sword.

### God Realized As Individual Consciousness Universally Brings the Reign of the Christ

Automatically a whole new consciousness of prayer evolves because now when a person who knows this truth prays, the first word that comes into his mind is omniscience, and with it comes a smile: "What have I to say to the All-knowing? What am I here for? Omniscience is the omnipotence, and this is the All-power, so I am certainly not here to get any power to do anything to some other power. This omnipotence is omnipresence, so I do not have to go anywhere for that." When we have finished with that, prayer becomes a listening attitude and in that altitude of prayer, that which is necessary comes through.

It may not come through in any way that we are aware of at the moment, but it will not be long before we will see the fruitage, and then we will say, "The Presence did go before me to 'make the crooked places straight.'[12] Omnipotence is omnipotence. That which appeared as the other power is not around. Omnipresence is the truth. Therefore, the truth I know in my consciousness is powerful in any city or country in the world. The omnipotence which is my consciousness is made manifest in Europe, Asia, or Africa, because it is my consciousness that is omniscience, omnipotence, and omnipresence, and it is a consciousness which does not have to be manipulated by human thought or power, but rather in quietness and in confidence it manifests itself."

All we have to do is sit quietly in a room and know this truth and it must function in what is called this world. So, in our world work, we must see that our consciousness is the power, but it must be consciously realized, and in our present state of development it has to be a specific activity. When the threat of war arises, the threat of strikes, or the threat of infection or contagion, at that moment we must specifically turn within. It will not be necessary in the ages to come when the Christ will be the realized consciousness of the individual. Then there will be no ground where infection, contagion, war, or hate can operate. As long as there is a human consciousness in which the illusions of sense can operate, the "ten righteous men" have to pray, and they must pray specifically at the time when the appearance touches their consciousness.

In the absolute it would be enough to say that God constitutes individual consciousness, but that will not do anything until the time when God is recognized as individual consciousness *universally* and Christ-government reigns on earth. To the extent that we have recognized God as individual consciousness and to the extent that we have recognized that spiritual power does not destroy anything, that it cannot be used but that it dispels illusion, to that extent are we individually Christ-governed or God-governed. Our individual realization of this truth helps to bring God's government on earth as it is in heaven.

For this reason when serious students are made aware of impending discord in their community, there is a need for immediate work. At other times, their world work must include the other side of the stick. They must not be fooled by good weather, good health, or good supply. They must consciously realize that they are not aiming toward achieving good supply, good health, or good government. They are concerned only with the middle path, Christ-harmony, Christ-supply, and Christ-weather.

Students must be alert not to get hooked on rejoicing in good humanhood, but must always remember that they are on the middle path. They are not here to change bad humanhood into good humanhood: they are to realize Christhood. This constitutes our "pearl."

These pearls of the Infinite Way are beyond price. They cannot be bought. No one, however wealthy, can hire a practitioner to keep him healthy, wealthy, and wise. No one can buy protection; no one can buy health. If those who express gratitude have any idea at all that they are buying God's favors or buying spiritual good, they might just as well keep their money. What is given to those engaged in this work is given out of pure gratitude, but if anyone has an idea that with the expression of gratitude he is buying something, he is mistaken. Our pearl cannot be purchased, except by inner struggle, nights of the soul, dark nights, some of them, because these truths that are brought forth from consciousness are not floating around for anybody and everybody to pick up. There have been too few who have caught them in the whole history of the world, and those few have been on the cross in one way or another.

Those who wish to bring forth pearls of wisdom from their consciousness will pay the price, but it will not be in dollars. The dollars they give will merely be the measure of their gratitude for what has happened.

## ACROSS THE DESK

The difference between humanhood and Christhood can be found in the two words *getting* and *letting*. As human beings, we are constantly driven to *get:* we get up in the morning, get breakfast, get to work, get lunch, get home, get to bed, all in order to get money to get food and clothing so that we can keep on getting to work. Everything appears to come from the outside, and in that belief human beings are enslaved to a life of getting.

The transition to our realized Christhood changes our life from one of getting to one of *letting*. We let that mind be in us which was also in Christ Jesus: we let "the imprisoned splendor escape." The whole purpose of our life changes as this enlightened awareness lifts consciousness.

The kingdom is within, not outside to get. Through meditation we enter that kingdom and let It flow out from our conscious oneness with God. We are then a blessing to all we meet. We are no longer in bondage to getting: we are released into the joy of letting.

TEACHING THE INFINITE WAY
"Freedom for Teacher, Practitioner, Patient, and Student"

"Teachers and practitioners give students the opportunity to come to them for instruction or healing. A spiritual teacher, however, is not only supposed to teach: he is supposed to reveal the hidden glories in a student's consciousness and the glorious nature of infinite individual consciousness. As the teacher helps to set his students free from their fears, free from two powers, free from dependency on 'man, whose breath is in his nostrils,'[13] they attain illumination.

"The student is illumined in proportion to his knowledge of specific principles. In his illumined state, he can walk up and down the world, and the evils do not touch him. If, then, he walks off by himself, the teacher should not be surprised because that is his prerogative. It would be sinful for a teacher to hold anyone to a membership. That would be holding him in further bondage, whereas the function of a spiritual teacher is to set students free.

"A teacher must not attempt to draw students to him or try to hold on to students. If a student wants to come today, the teacher is to give whatever he can; if students do not want to come tomorrow, that is not the teacher's business, because students are evolving according to their individual light.

"Those Infinite Way teachers who have study centers or activities should make the tapes, books, meetings and classes available to all, but no teacher should urge attendance upon them. They should encourage students to own books for study and reference, but they must be careful not to become proselyters or merely book salesmen. A teacher may present a lesson to students, but he has no right to compel them to study it.

"Teachers and practitioners are merely serving as a light; it is up to the students to what extent they wish to avail themselves of that light. Those who are hungering and thirsting after truth will, of course, avail themselves of it to the greatest degree, and the teacher can do nothing about the others.

"How many people are there who have wonderful healings and then write and say, 'Thank you'! They are not interested in anything of a spiritual nature until they need another healing. There is no use trying to tell them that they are wasting their life, that sooner or later this thing is not going to work for them. They have to find that out for themselves.

"A teacher always gives a student his freedom. In his ignorance the student may use that freedom to harm himself, but that the teacher cannot help. It is better that he harm himself as a free person than that the teacher protect him and keep him in bondage, depending on the teacher's consciousness forever.

"All this comes under the heading of illumination. The illumined consciousness is one that is gaining or has gained its freedom by virtue of knowing the infinite nature of individual consciousness, the omnipresence of it, the omnipotence of it, and the omniscience of it."

Joel S. Goldsmith, *1963 Instructions for Teaching the Infinite Way.*

*Chapter Six*

# Not Appearances But *Is*

*T*he *Infinite Way*[1] clearly states that a problem cannot be met on the level of the problem. Ninety percent of the failures in healing arise from ignorance of the meaning of that statement. When, from every human standpoint, a person appears to be dying, the immediate thought would probably be, "What are we going to do to save his life?" When a person talks of unhappiness in his marriage, our first thought runs to "What can be done to make the marriage a happy one?" When a person is unemployed, immediately there comes to mind, "What can we think or know to bring employment to him?"

All this is a barrier to success in healing because no Infinite Way student is a healer of disease or of sin, nor is he an employment agency or a marriage counselor. He does not meet a problem on the level of the problem, so no matter what the person says about his problem, the Infinite Way student is not hearing it, and certainly he is not answering it because that would put him in the realm of a counselor or doctor. No problem can ever be met on the level of the problem.

## *The Fluctuating Nature of Humanhood*

The picture that confronts us is that there is sick humanhood and well humanhood, sinful humanhood and pure humanhood, living humanhood and dead humanhood, and the purpose of the medical and ministerial world is to take that bad or erroneous humanhood and put it over onto the good side. But that does not in any way enter into our ministry. The function of our ministry is to ignore everything that is being told us about sin, disease, death, lack, limitation, and politics, and to go down through the center, through what we call the middle path. We do not think in terms of what a wonderful society it would be if only all politicians were honest, if everybody were humanly well, or if everybody had a sufficient income.

We have had periods in American history where, on the whole, conditions were very good. The country made tremendous progress; the standard of living was steadily rising; and employment was high. But these conditions did not continue. From the Civil War to World War I, the only scrap the United States had was the Spanish American War, which, considering the size of it, was really a skirmish. Since the First World War, however, there has been nothing but war all over the world on a huge scale. So even if we could be as wise as the founding fathers who brought forth a free nation and then gave it a constitution to keep it free, we would have no assurance as to what the next generation or the one after that would do to tear it apart.

If we could make all our friends well, how would we go about keeping them well? If we could be sure that all the sinners and alcoholics who came to us could be immediately transformed, what would we do about keeping them that way? Nothing, because good humanhood can become bad humanhood, and bad humanhood can become good humanhood. This is a continually fluctuating process, generation after generation.

### Spiritual Awakening Is the Goal

Making the sick well is not the function of the Infinite Way, nor is it making the sinful pure, nor turning corrupt politics into honest politics. Our function is to awaken to the truth of the spiritual nature of God, man's spiritual nature, and the spiritual nature of the universe that God created.

"In him we live, and move, and have our being."[2] We live, and move, and have our being in the divine consciousness which is "of purer eyes than to behold iniquity,"[3] into which nothing can enter "that defileth. . . or maketh a lie."[4] So we must, in some measure, be able to realize that nothing a person tells us about himself will we believe, not even if he tells us something good.

True, we can be grateful if a person has a healing, but we cannot rejoice merely in the healing because we do not know what he will come back with next week. Sometimes one devil is cleared out only to make room for seven to enter.[5] Our rejoicing occurs when an individual awakens to the spiritual nature and source of life and begins to follow the spiritual path.

Our work has nothing to do with whether a person has a claim of sickness, sin, or lack. Once he is in tune with the Infinite, receptive to the voice and aware of It, to that extent our function has been completed with him. We lead a person and lift him in consciousness to the ability to find God, God-power, and God-presence, and to be receptive to spiritual impartations.

When we are engaged in healing work, we are not concerned with whether the fever or the lump goes down. We are not concerned with whether a person can walk or whether he is in a mental institution. We are not trying to turn these conditions into their opposite. We live, and move, and have our being in an inner communion in which the "still small voice"[6] reveals to us the nature of God, the nature of God's universe, and the nature of God's being and man's being.

## *Refuse To "Join" the Issue*

By dwelling in this middle path, we are not trying to meet the problem on the level of the problem. We are not trying to turn an unhappy marriage into a happy one, lack into abundance, unemployment into employment, or an alcoholic into a non-alcoholic. To do that would be like going out to fight windmills. It would be resisting evil and fighting the appearance. Rather do we refrain from entering into a combat.

In legal battles, the issue must be drawn. One side says, "This is the way it is," and the other side says, "No, that is not it." Thus the issue is joined, and unless an issue is joined, there is no case at law. Somebody has to say, "Yes," and somebody has to say, "No." If both sides are in agreement there is no case, and one cannot go to court.

When an appearance is presented to us—person, place, thing, circumstance, or condition—and we deny it, the issue is joined. Now we are ready to fight it out. But if we brush aside the appearance and turn to the realization of the spiritual nature of God and His creation, of His being expressed as man, we will have a revelation of spiritual being—not mental healing, not metaphysical healing, but spiritual healing, and there is no power involved in this whatsoever. We do not want a God-power to do something to something. We are abiding in the nature of spiritual cause and creation.

## *Focus Attention on the Things of God*

Keep your conversation, even your silent conversation with yourself, in heaven. Keep your mind focused on God, the spirit, the invisible. Then take some phase of God, whether it is life, love, substance, or law, and keep pondering on God as the only law of the universe, thereby annihilating all sense of human law: legal law, material law, medical law, or atomic law. Think of

God as the source of all life. Thus "every word that proceedeth out of the mouth of God"[7] becomes more and more that life eternal in your experience.

As you keep pondering these things you finally come to a place where thought automatically stops. There is nothing left to think about, and peace descends. In that peace you wait for the voice to speak to you, for the assurance to come, for inspiration of one sort or another. In that way you develop the ability to be receptive to the divine consciousness. You tap the source of love divine, life divine, truth divine, the source of all inspiration. But you tap it only when you go beyond the realm of thinking.

## The Unknowingness of Wisdom

There is a spiritual presence at the center of your being and mine, and this spiritual presence is empowered from on High with all the power of the Godhead. It is not a little bit of power only, not merely a spark of power. It is a power derived from God. It gives you power to forgive sin and to heal disease. A person endowed with that power from on High can say, "Rise, pick up your bed and walk. What hinders you? Pick up your bed and walk." That is not a person talking. It is Spirit Itself being voiced through the avenue of individual consciousness. If the Father does not say it, a person could say, "Rise," forever and a day, and nothing would happen.

Healing work is the product of a divine inspiration or illumination that flows up from the center of our being. It is a living experience within the soul. Anyone who tries to do healing work just because he has read all the words in a book or because he knows the correct statements of truth to make, will fail, even though at the beginning he may have a little temporary measure of success. Healing work is not a product of your mind or mine: it is not the product of thought: it far transcends anything that you or I may know. If this were not true, the Master would not have said, "I can of mine own self do nothing."[8] Even with all he knew, he, himself, could not have done the great things he accomplished. He recognized that he of himself could not do anything; it was the Father within him that did the work.

So as long as you of yourself can do nothing, there must be a period—even if a split second—in which you know nothing, are nothing, desire nothing, but become a vacuum in order that It, the word of God, may spring forth through your lips.

Moses was slow of speech, but the Lord promised that He would put the words in Moses' mouth, and He did. If you are called before a magistrate, you do not need clever thoughts, wisecracks, or profound knowledge. You need the humble faith that of your own self you can do nothing, but that there is within your being that which can impart Itself to you in all Its wisdom, in all Its glory, in all Its power.

### *Develop the Consciousness of* Is

When you are called upon for help, do not hesitate to sit down and hold up the word *is* in front of you: *is, is, is.* It is as if you were to think, "There *is* something here, but I do not know what it is or who it is. It claims to be a person and a condition, but I know nothing about those things. I do not know how to pray. I do not know how to meditate. I must let the Spirit bear witness with my spirit. I must let the Spirit make intercession for me. So I do not know who this is, what this is, or why this is. I only know that before me there is an *is.* There is something; there is somebody. Now, Father, take over and enlighten me." From the depths of your withinness will come some kind of a peace-be-still to the situation, some kind of an assurance, and you will begin to see harmony.

When somebody says he is a sick human being, a poor human being, or an unemployed human being, you must remember that you have been told by the spirit of truth in you not to judge after appearances. You cannot judge what or who is before you, and so you use the word *is*. You do know that there is an *is* here: something is here, someone is here. What is it? Who is it? What is the truth about it? Then you turn within and let the divine impartation unfold. You let Wisdom reveal Itself and watch what happens.

There is not only an intuitive sense but a higher spiritual sense that reveals what we must know without thinking or reasoning. When you sit down, you do not affirm the truth; you do not deny the error. You wait, and the light from within, the illumination, the "click," or the release comes. You do not know anything with your human mind; you do not know what has happened, yet in the course of time you receive word that the healing has taken place.

Knowing the truth is necessary only in order to have something to cling to within that gives you the human assurance of a superhuman presence and power. As you watch this, you will observe that the human mind is not necessary in spiritual healing work or in spiritual living, but that there is a divine truth which comes through to do the work.

## Go Beyond the Appearance to Is

Let us suppose that you have never seen a little rosebud before so you do not know what it is. There is only one thing that you know about it: you know that it is. You do not know that it is a flower. You do not know that it is a bud. You do not know anything about it. You've never seen anything like it before, and so you know nothing about it except one thing. You know that something is. The only thing of which you are certain is that something is here. What it is you do not know. Why it is you do not know.

But you can take the word *is*. Of that you are certain. Then close your eyes and become very still. If you do that, it will not be long before an impartation comes to you from within that this is a flower, a bud, a rose, or that this is something in the kingdom of God. What it is will be revealed to you, and it will be revealed not by any human knowing since we are assuming that you have no human knowledge of it. But it will be revealed by a higher consciousness which we call the Spirit Itself.

If you were to judge by appearances when called on for help, you would be continuously faced with universal medical theories, symptoms, diagnoses, and beliefs. If you turned to metaphysical books, what would you find? Statements that you are spiritual, that you are perfect, that you are harmonious. And what good would that do? You are still complaining about your aches and pains even after you have read how spiritual you are. You might even have pages pointed out for you to read so that you, yourself, could read how spiritual you are.

Instead of delving around in what is known humanly about a person and instead of delving around in books to find out what is spiritually known about him, go into the silence. Retreat inside your own being and frankly admit that you know nothing. Jesus not only said that he could of his own self do nothing, but he even said that if he talked of himself he bore witness to a lie. You know far less than Jesus, and he knew that he knew nothing.

You have to say or admit to yourself that you know nothing about the situation; you know nothing about the person; you know nothing about this claim; and you certainly know nothing about God's kingdom. So you turn to the Father for light, for wisdom, for enlightenment, for peace, and for truth. As you learn to sit in this receptive attitude, into your waiting consciousness comes some assurance. If you can have the assurance from God that the person who has asked for help is His beloved, you are sure everything is all right and that he is in God's care. You cannot bring forth any healing through reading such a statement in a book, but when the Father, Itself, speaks, then you may be assured that all is well.

After a person has said that he is well or better, you still do not know what happened. You know nothing about the operation of the Spirit in your experience. You only know that with Its assurance comes a measure of release or freedom to you.

### The Mystical Consciousness of the Infinite Way

This is what we call the Infinite Way consciousness. It is the consciousness that does not fight the appearance and does not try to change it. All Infinite Way writings tell us over and over again that we are not to try to change humanhood, and yet, consciously, subconsciously, or unconsciously, we are all trying to do just that, are we not? We are so happy when someone tells us the pain has stopped, when as a matter of fact it might be far better if that pain continued until the person was compelled to awaken. That is why a problem is not a problem: it is an opportunity.

Why should a human being who is well, moderately happy, and moderately successful give his life to the spiritual path? Not only is there no reason, but a human being will not do this. That, a practitioner recognizes by what goes on in his practice. As soon as the patient is well he tells the practitioner to stop work and bids him good-bye until he needs help for the next claim. He is perfectly happy in his new-found human health and wealth. At least eighty or ninety percent are. Instead of telling a practitioner to stop when a person has been healed, he should be saying, "Begin! Now lead me to that consciousness so that I can maintain it for myself, my family, and all who may be led to me."

In proportion as a person permits himself to be God-governed, his life is God-governed. But he cannot merely say, "Oh, yes, God, I am ready for You to govern me." That is not giving one's self to God-government. Giving one's self to God's government means accepting the laws of God and acting out from them. That means that insofar as a person finds it possible, he must consciously remember that love is the secret of the spiritual life. Unless he is loving his neighbor as himself, forgiving, doing for "the least of these, my brethren,"[9] he is not accepting God's government.

The most advanced step in the message of the Infinite Way is not to meet a problem on the level of the problem. Such a step can be imparted only by a person who has caught its significance. At that stage, the Infinite Way student is at the highest mystical point, having lost all interest in changing negative or bad humanhood into good humanhood. He is interested in one thing only: the reign of God on earth. That is all. He is concerned only with the realization that God's kingdom is "on earth, as it is in heaven."[10] Heaven and earth are one: heaven, the invisible cause, and earth, the visible manifestation of heaven, but always one.

## ACROSS THE DESK

Consciousness expresses and fulfills Itself, so we need never attempt to manipulate anything in the human picture. We are beholders watching the activity of God express as our life, our supply, our health, our relationships, our peace, and our fulfillment.

If our work is not the fulfillment of our destiny, it will leave us: we need not leave it. If our home is not God-bestowed and God-governed, it will leave us and take form as something more satisfying. Inharmonious relationships will fall away.

We are not doers: we are watchers, beholders. In being beholders we turn within to watch God being.

We need never run from anything. We need never try to change anything in the picture. We face each experience, every picture, and let the outflow of God-consciousness take over, dissolving the hypnotic illusion of the human picture and revealing reality.

### Teaching the Infinite Way
"What Makes a Practitioner or Teacher"

"As a practitioner or a teacher you cannot permit anyone to believe that you have some kind of an inside influence with God which will enable you to get health, supply, divorce, or a marriage for a person.

"The moment you begin to explain to a student or patient that your function is to reveal the kingdom of God, you have begun to teach, and the moment he has accepted that and you begin to meditate for him that the grace of God be revealed within him, you are a practitioner. Whether you are recognized as a teacher or practitioner, you become one in the moment that anyone comes to you seeking what you have to give. Being engaged in the work as a teacher or practitioner professionally merely means that a person not only has attained sufficient consciousness to do this work, but also that he is sufficiently free of business or family ties so that he can give a great portion of his time to those who come to him. Those who become known as practitioners and teachers will never, by any manner of means, represent the number of those who are capable of performing such a service if they had sufficient freedom from other cares and responsibilities.

"Any student who has come to recognize and realize the nature of God, the nature of prayer, the nature of man, and the nature of error is a teacher or practitioner, but *only*, of course, after he has been called upon to perform that function. It is folly to seek to be a practitioner or teacher. Such an ambition cannot succeed. That is why I remind students so often that it is deadly to be a 'do-gooder'; it is deadly to want to save the world; it is deadly to want to be a teacher or a practitioner. The only life-giving substance there is, is the desire to know God aright. This alone is worthwhile.

"Regardless of how good your wishes may be, you never will

be able to help this world or anyone in it until you yourself have attained spiritually. Leave the world alone, and if it must burn itself up, let it, while you go about your business of attaining spiritual consciousness. You will find that having attained that consciousness, you will be busier than you would like to be because the world will then beat a pathway to your door. That is what happens. Wherever the light is, the darkness gravitates there to be dispelled."

### Attaining the Healing Consciousness

"There are only two ways in which the healing consciousness can be attained. One is by an act of Grace, which means that we do not know how it happened or why, but out of the clear it did happen. My experience shows that the healing consciousness comes to very few persons that way. All the others attain the healing consciousness through the practice of specific principles.

"There can be no rules laid down or any regulations governing the development of spiritual consciousness. With one it may take place in an instant through the realization of just one principle, while with another it may come about only after years and years of living with the principles until one, two, or three of these principles begin to register.

"Years ago an early student of metaphysics became known as a great healer. He did not tell his students his secret because he realized that they could not grasp it even if he were to tell them. But one of his students was determined to learn the reason for his success. She was in a situation at one time that made it possible for her to say to him, 'I know that you have a secret that is responsible for your great healing works. I must know what is it.'

"He said, 'Yes, I do have a secret and I would like to tell it to you, but it will not do you any good.'

"'Oh, I do not believe that! I must know it.'

"Her persistence won out for her, and eventually he said, 'All right, I am going to tell it to you. I was taught that mortal mind is a term denoting nothingness. So, when any error is presented to me I just say, "Mortal mind," and forget it.' He was right: she could not grasp it.

"The message of the Infinite Way has as its major healing principle the nature of error. If you can grasp the truth that all error, regardless of whether it is individual or collective, whether it concerns a person or a tidal wave, is actually nothing but the universal belief in two powers, you are a good practitioner and you will have excellent results. That has always been its principle, and still there are very few successful practitioners. Why? Because the belief in two powers is so firmly implanted in human consciousness that we are not able to look at a form of error and say, 'It is neither good nor evil.' We are determined to get rid of it, overcome it, or rise above it, or we are determined to try to get the power of God to do something to it.

"To be a teacher or practitioner of the Infinite Way does not mean that you have power to heal people of disease, of lack, or of discordant relationships. It means that you have attained the recognition of the illusory nature of what is presented to you as a problem. It does not mean that you are so close to God that God, through you, will do something for mankind. Heaven forbid that God should be so localized as to be personal to anybody. To be a teacher, to be a practitioner, or to be able to help those who come to you means that you have attained an awareness of the principles of the Infinite Way and that through constantly living with them, studying them, and putting them into practice, your consciousness has evolved to that place where, when you are asked for help, you, too, can say, 'illusion,' and then go back to sleep.

"The kingdom of God is intact. Spiritual man has not degenerated into a mortal, and mortal man is never going to be lifted up into the status of a spiritual being. What happens is that the teacher or practitioner has attained the capacity to see the spiritual son of God and not believe the appearance, whether it testifies to sin, disease, lack, or limitation. This is a spiritual healer, not the one who prays to God that you be healed. The spiritual healer can look you right in the eye and say, 'I know who you are. You are God, Itself, individualized.' And then, to this appearance of sin, disease, false appetite, or lack, be able to say, 'That is the illusion: that is what would fool me into trying to do something to nothing.'

"Remember the illustration given in many Infinite Way classes about going out to the desert and seeing a big body of water on the road ahead of you. What are you going to do? Bring a hose and pump it off? That is what the 'do-gooders' would do. No, you are going to look at it and say, 'It is an illusion,' and drive right through it, not even seeking God's help."

## Christhood, Not Human Good

"Spiritual healing is predicated on a further revelation of the Infinite Way, and that is that prayer and meditation are not to be used for increasing humanhood or improving it. That is not the way. Infinite Way teachers and practitioners must develop the consciousness within themselves that knows they are not trying to improve somebody's humanhood: they are not trying to reduce a fever; they are not trying to remove germs; they are not trying to provide better employment or happier households.

"The Infinite Way teacher or practitioner must have as his goal the realization of the Christ, the realization of spiritual identity. It is true that with this realization all things are added, but you and I have nothing to do with that. In the Infinite Way you do not deal with good health; you do not deal with supply and happiness: you deal with the revelation of the Christ as individual selfhood. This is the seed of truth. Then this seed embodied in your consciousness, kept there secretly and sacredly, bears fruit, and the fruitage is peace, prosperity, health, wholeness, happiness. But you do not have those things, not any more than Peter and John had them at the Temple Gate Beautiful: 'Silver and gold have I none.'[11] Then what do you have? The spirit of God.

"Those who come to you for help will nearly always come for the fruits. Then begins the process of re-education: 'Yes, I will take up work for you at once, but remember, I am seeking for you the realization of God, the activity of divine grace, and then the things will be added.' In the beginning you may not be able to tell new students all this. It has to be given to them very gently, but eventually you must lead them to the recognition of that fact, through revealing the nature of God, the nature of prayer, the nature of error, and ultimately the nature of man.

"As a rule the next point can only be imparted after years of work, unless it be to some unusual student who is spiritually opened and capable of receiving it sooner. The nature of God and the nature of man are one and the same, because God and man are one and the same: there are not two. There is not God *and* man! Actually God is individual man. 'He that seeth me seeth him that sent me.'[12] Why? Because I and the Father are one, and therefore, all that God is, I am. All that the Father has is mine. When you say, *'I,'* you mean God because the nature of God has been revealed as the *I* of man."

### How a Patient Experiences Healing

"When we say that disease is an illusion, it does not mean that you have a disease in your body and that we are going to get rid of it. It means that it is a mental misperception which does not exist in or on your body, and the recognition of it as illusion dispels the picture. Poverty is not a condition of your pocketbook: the condition is the poverty of your mind. There is no such thing as poverty of pocketbook, because equally every one of us owns all there is on earth. 'The earth is the Lord's, and the fulness thereof,'[13] and 'Son, thou art ever with me, and all that I have is thine.'[14]

"As you look out at the world, do not declare that it is an illusion, but rather that the erroneous concept of it that you are entertaining is the illusion. Any erroneous picture that you are accepting is the illusion, and therefore the illusion exists in your mental misperception, not in the external world. If you grasp the point that an illusion cannot be externalized, that it can never exist externally, then you will understand the Infinite Way and its healing principle.

"Suppose that somebody told you that two times two is five. Would you try to change that externally? No, because there never has been such a thing as two times two is five externally. You correct it within yourself, and because my Self is your Self, you who have brought your Self to my Self receive the benefit. The Infinite Way principle is that any truth realized in the practitioner's consciousness becomes the law unto the patient or student who has brought himself to that consciousness. Never does the practitioner project his thought to a patient or student, never! He does not use the word *you* in any treatment, prayer, or meditation. It is always whatever truth he can realize. Then the truth he realizes becomes the law unto the patient because he has brought himself to the practitioner's consciousness.

"In the spiritual kingdom there is neither time nor space. So neither time nor space enters into a spiritual healing. The only thing that enters into a spiritual healing is consciousness, and the moment a person attunes himself to the Christ-consciousness, the healing should appear. Very often the healing comes to a person long before the practitioner receives the written, telephoned, or cabled message, and sometimes even before it has been mailed.

"You would be surprised how many patients claim they can tell just when the practitioner received their message, because that is when they received their healing. Of course, it did not happen that way at all because they had no way of knowing when the message arrived. Sometimes there is a difference in time from one place to another; sometimes it is a day before or a day after, and sometimes the practitioner is not even at home when the message comes, so nobody has any real way of knowing when the message is received. But because in their own minds they decided that when he got the message he would do something about it and they would be healed, they made that a law unto themselves.

"There are others who wait for an answer to reach them, and if it does not reach them fast enough, they write and ask where the answer is because they are waiting for their healing. They are in a hurry to get their answer, as if receiving a piece of paper from a practitioner were going to give them their healing. If there is to be a healing through a practitioner it has to be an activity of his consciousness. Why wait, then, to receive a piece of paper? The moment a patient brings himself to the practitioner's consciousness, whatever is operating in that realized consciousness becomes the law unto the patient.

"The moment students attune themselves to any practitioner's realized consciousness, in that instant they have a right to expect the answer, even if they never get a message, because the healing has nothing to do with letters, telegrams, telephones, or cables; it has nothing to do with reaching human ears or human eyes. Mind is not a healer. It is the consciousness that has developed and evolved, and the truth is that the consciousness of a practitioner who knows this truth is omnipresent where the patient is. His consciousness is omnipresent because he realizes: I and the Father are one, therefore I and the Father are right where the patient is. At the moment he lifts his consciousness to the practitioner, the *I* of the practitioner is instantaneously there."

Joel S. Goldsmith, *1963 London Work.*

*Chapter Seven*

# Material Sense of Demonstration or the Unfoldment of Grace

Two aspects of life confront us on the spiritual path: the material sense of life, made up of good and evil, with more evil than good and the good sometimes turning to evil, and the spiritual consciousness of life which is neither good nor evil but is wholly spiritual, wholly the offspring or activity of God.

In reality we are not dealing with two powers. We are dealing with material sense and its claim to power and with spiritual consciousness which is the only power. Along with the rest of the world we are being faced with a material sense of world: material powers and mental powers. But having learned something of the nature of spiritual power and spiritual reality, we can reveal the nothingness of this material sense of world. The Master gave us a glimpse of this in his statement, "My kingdom is not of this world."[1] In other words, the spiritual kingdom is not of the material world.

When normal, ordinary, material methods are used to get the things a person desires, wants, or needs, and these fail, he turns to Spirit and tries to get from Spirit improved matter and improved material conditions. He tries to use the power of Spirit to nullify the powers of mind and matter. Therein lies the first mistake.

At one time mind was looked upon as a power over matter, but the impossibility of this is evident to those who realize that what the world calls matter really is mind. The substance of matter is mind. Matter is the visible form of invisible mind. It is not that mind is a power over matter or that thought is a power over material conditions. It is that mind itself constitutes matter and material conditions, and the more mind is used for good purposes, the more good matter appears because mind and matter are one.

The more evil or error there is in the mind, the more erroneous matter there is because mind and matter are one. Mind is the substance and matter is the form, just as glass is the substance of a tumbler, but the tumbler is the form. So mind is the substance of matter, and on the level of mind, of this world, we have good and we have evil.

### The World Seeks Solutions in More Power and Things

Finding no answers to its problems on the material level, the world has sought something greater than itself, something greater than man. So it created gods which under the ancient Hebrews became one God. But, it really was not God because in the Old Testament God is looked upon as a great spiritual power which can be used in a material universe and can be used for good and for evil: to destroy our enemies or to get food and water when they are needed.

Jesus pointed out the error of that when he was tempted to use spiritual power for bread. His answer was, "Man shall not live by bread alone,"[2] revealing that it is useless to go to a spiritual God for material bread, because man actually lives by the Word.

The Master again pointed out how wrong it is to turn to God for power over any material condition when he said, "Take no thought for your life, what ye shall eat; neither for the body, what ye shall put on. . . . Seek ye the kingdom of God,"[3] the realm of Spirit. Then the things will be added unto you. Do not try through the power of Spirit to control material conditions. This was the mistake of the ancients, and this is the mistake of modern religion which is trying to turn to a superpower called Spirit, God, divine Love, and thereby get more matter in one form or another or change a diseased body into a healthy body.

The use of *materia medica* is certainly right for those living out from the physical sense of life, and the use of mind-power is right for those in the mental sense of life, but both of these deal with one power over another power, with changing one condition into another condition. In doing that, a person is maintaining himself in the world, but this world has nothing to do with *My* kingdom, the spiritual kingdom of God.

### *Laws of Matter or Mind Do Not Operate in Spiritual Consciousness*

The purpose of the Infinite Way is not to find a power whereby to control men, conditions, or effects, but to attain God-consciousness, and thereby discover that the so-called laws of both matter and mind are not laws. They are laws only on their own level, but they do not function when a person is living out from the realm of Spirit.

As long as we are living in the world of mind and matter, if there is an epidemic we are just as much subject to the disease as anybody else. Whether or not we contract it might depend on the state of our system at that particular time. Once we attain a measure of that "mind. . . which was also in Christ Jesus,"[4] which is spiritual consciousness, the laws of matter and the laws of mind do not operate. That is why the spiritual healer can heal. It is not because he can remove power from germs or render them powerless. No, he leaves the realm of germs and rises into the Spirit where there are no germs and there are no powers.

Jesus' statement, "I am come that they might have life, and that they might have it more abundantly,"⁵ does not mean that a person comes along to destroy germs, growths, or rheumatism, or to increase crops. It means that *I,* the Spirit of God within, is come that we might have life, and that we might have life more abundantly.

What form does that life take? Since there have been thousands of years of trying to use the power of the Unknown to improve this world, we all unconsciously are attempting to get the grace of God to do something to our human world. If someone says that it will not work and that we have to leave the human world for *My* kingdom, the response often is, "That is too nebulous. How do I know what I'll find when I get there?"

It is like telling a person "Do not fear death. Death is only the closing of one door and the opening of another."

"Yes, but you can't tell me what's going to be behind that other door, so I'll be satisfied with the door I have even if I have to stay locked up in prison the rest of my life. I'd rather do that than explore the next world."

So the disease-ridden person would rather suffer for years and years than to take a chance on exploring what is behind that closed door. It really cannot be anything too terrifying because it has been provided that everybody in the world has to go through that door. It would be hard to believe that everybody is sentenced to something uncomfortable.

### *Metaphysics Attempts to Improve Humanhood; Mysticism Rises to Another Dimension*

Here is the dividing line between all metaphysics and mysticism. Metaphysics is turning to a power to improve the human estate: mysticism is leaving behind the human estate, even if it is good, and trying to pierce the veil that sees into that other universe called "My kingdom."

What is health in *My* kingdom? What is abundance in *My* kingdom? There is no use matching up health with a heart that works, with liver and lungs, and certainly no use matching up abundance with so many dollars because it will not work. What is harmony in the spiritual realm? That is the goal of our meditation, not contacting God so that material conditions can be improved, not contacting God to prevent somebody from dying, or to stop his pain. The goal is seeking the awareness.

For this reason, in prayer, meditation, or treatment, we never permit the patient to come into our thought. When a person asks, "Will you give me help?" it may relieve his mind to tell us that he wants help for rheumatism, marital trouble, business trouble, or some other trouble. We pay no attention to that, however, because there is nothing we could do about it even if we could repeat what he said verbatim. So we let it go in one ear and out the other because we recognize that what is being told us is something that has to do with this world. Actually it would be just as erroneous if the person were telling us how happy and prosperous he is. So we pay no attention to it, and for that reason we do not gloat when the patient gets well, because he is still telling us about a happening in this world.

If we are grateful it is because we have caught a glimpse of the spiritual universe and its grace. That is quite different. If a person is ill, asks for help, and gets it, we are grateful. We are not grateful that he has health: we are grateful that we have glimpsed the spiritual kingdom and brought it to his experience. At least now he is experiencing something of harmony of a spiritual nature.

If we were grateful that a person became well, tomorrow he could call up and say, "I am sick again." But once he has glimpsed the nature of the spiritual kingdom, he will have less and less reason to experience physical discords.

So when an individual telephones, writes, or comes to see us, and pours out his problem, we recognize it as merely the hypnotism of the senses. We do not personalize it: we recognize the impersonal nature of it as mass hypnotism, and then forget who it is who has written, cabled, telephoned, or is sitting before us. Forgetting him and his problems, we turn within, remembering that *I,* God, the Christ, stands at the door of our consciousness and knocks. We turn within and say, "Speak, Lord; enter." We keep the inner ear open as if we were waiting to receive the word of God. Even if it is not audible, we will know when we receive it. As far as we are concerned, that ends the treatment, prayer, or meditation.

If we try to heal, employ, or enrich somebody, we are indulging in the very material sense that brought on the problem. But when we can turn away from the appearance, turn within, and seek the Light, the Word, we are in spiritual consciousness. We meditate not for the purpose of healing or employing a person, but for the purpose of catching a glimpse of *My* kingdom. When we are able to catch even a glimpse of that kingdom, he tells us that the pain or the disease is gone, that there is happiness in the home, or that there is a separation—whatever will result in harmony.

But let us not be grateful for the healing, and let not the patient be grateful for the healing. The gratitude must be that the kingdom of God has been realized on earth, that we have caught a glimpse of the fourth dimensional realm. In the fourth dimensional or spiritual realm, all is harmony. There is no darkness there. "God is light and in him is no darkness at all.[6]. . . In thy presence is fulness of joy,"[7] no discord, no inharmony. So what we have proven is that we have been lifted up into His presence, Its presence, *The* presence. Gratitude should always be that we have witnessed the kingdom of God on earth as it is in heaven, not just for a healing, for justice, or for abundance.

If we are grateful for a healing, for supply, or for justice, we would have only good material sense instead of bad material sense. But it would still be material sense. When we abide in the kingdom, we seek and find the kingdom of God. We do not have degrees: we do not have health and sickness, life and death, abundance and lack. We have spiritual grace, a sufficiency of health, wealth, justice, and mercy.

## Spiritual Rightness and Wholeness

So it is, then, that we are meeting the appearances and effects of material sense, and dealing with the attainment of the kingdom of God on earth. "Whatsoever a man soweth, that shall he also reap. For he that soweth to his flesh shall of the flesh reap corruption; but he that soweth to the Spirit shall of the Spirit reap life everlasting."[8] That means that if we keep giving power to matter and wanting to change forms of matter, we are sowing to the flesh. When we sow to the Spirit, we are seeking the kingdom of God and His righteousness, spiritual righteousness.

What is spiritual righteousness? What is spiritual wholeness? It has nothing to do with a physical body, a material pocketbook, or a human home. What did Jesus mean by seeking first the kingdom of God and his righteousness, the realm of spiritual rightness, His form of rightness? When we can answer that, we discover an entirely new world, the world that is *My* kingdom, not this world.

## Impersonalizing God

All of the spiritual kingdom is within us. We do not go to holy mountains, holy temples, or holy teachers for it. We go to those places and persons merely to learn that it is within. If we go there and come away with the belief that it is there, we leave it there when we leave. Orthodoxy personalizes God and claims that He walked the earth two thousand years ago and that sometime He is going to come back. Where does that leave us with this world of war, famine, drought, and man's inhumanity to man? If that is true, there is nothing we can do about it until God gets back to earth.

The freedom of the Infinite Way comes in the impersonalization of God, the acknowledgment that before there was Judaism, before there was Buddhism, before there was Christianity, before there was any *ism,* there was God. That same God still is, and we do not have to have faith in anything because faith implies believing in something of which we have no knowledge. That is ignorance, superstition, paganism. We might believe in telephones, but that would not help us make a telephone call. We have to have the experience. Otherwise it is in the realm of fantasy.

### *Demonstrate the Kingdom*

There is nothing impossible about attaining the spiritual kingdom. It comes without money, without price, or without going any place. It is to be experienced within us. We do not even have to be good to experience it. We do not work with persons in prisons and tell them first to get good and then we will heal them and give them spiritual truth, and ultimately that will make them free. No, we bring to them the experience of God, and then they find their goodness or their freedom.

So it is that we do not require a student to read so many pages of so many books every day or hear so many tapes every day. If the reading of the books, the hearing of the tapes, or having class would bring the kingdom closer to a person, then he should do just that. But remember those are only the bridges over which a person is traveling to the experience. It is the experience that does the work, not the words in any book or in any Bible. When we make contact through our meditation with the Spirit within us, we have the experience which reveals the nature of the spiritual kingdom. Then when we look at our human experience it is harmonious, no longer really a human experience, but the product of our spiritual experience.

When we hear the word of God, and food, housing, and transportation come, we know that we did not demonstrate these things: we demonstrated the spirit of God and that took form as the needed things of the moment.

The word of God takes form. For Elijah it took the form of food when he was in the wilderness without food. With Moses it took the form of manna falling from the sky and water from the rocks. With Jesus it took the form of the multiplication of the loaves and fishes. Religionists, however, make the mistake of trying to demonstrate effects. They are trying to multiply loaves and fishes, increase their supply, and it cannot be done. The only demonstration there is must be the demonstration of the presence of God. That is what Moses, Elijah, and Jesus demonstrated. None of those men was a trickster or a magician. Each one was a God inspired and God realized man. God realization takes the form of the things we have need of, whether it is justice in a courtroom, whether it is an election that should be rightfully decided, whether it is health, increased business, or whatever it may be.

### Crucifying Our Do-Gooding Sense

If we try to work in the realm of form, we are in material sense, manipulating effects, changing evil to good, and trying to be miracle workers. Sometimes we succeed and build a reputation of being a miracle worker and then end up on a crucifix because that is the fate of all miracle workers. That is the crucifixion that comes when we build a big reputation and then somebody tears it down.

The spiritual crucifixion comes when we attempt to give up all miracle works. We crucify ourselves when someone asks for help and we train ourselves not to try to reduce the fever or the lump, not to try to overcome deafness and blindness. In that restraint we are crucifying personal sense, our do-gooding sense.

We are seeking the realization of God, seeking to hear the word of God, to witness the light and the grace of God. All the time a person is reminding us that the lump is getting bigger, the pain is getting stronger, or the blindness is getting worse, we are crucifying the personal sense of self inside that wants to be helpful. We refuse to give way to the temptation to turn stones into bread. Instead, we are going to be still and know that *I* in the midst of us is God. *I* in the midst of us is mighty. *I* in the midst of us is the secret of the spiritual kingdom of harmony, peace, joy, and glory, and we are seeking His rightness, not the patient's rightness nor his health.

Then when that touch of the Spirit comes, we are still. Sometimes It smiles inside of us, "Foolish child, trying to be a miracle worker!" Then we get at peace, and the patient says, "Oh, a miracle has happened." Ah, but the miracle was not the healing: the miracle was that you or I experienced God. Why you or I out of all this world? We do not know the reason, but when we experience God, miracles take place out in the world. But let us not become hypnotized by miracles.

I have to warn our students over and over again that the moment they begin to be successful in the healing ministry, they will know financial prosperity such as they have never known before. Then they have to be wise because they can lose their whole demonstration if they think that the money is a gift of God or the grace of God. The grace of God is the Spirit they attain. The rest is just the added things. It does not make any difference if that money comes or goes. Whatever they need will be immediately available. His grace is omnipresent.

### Tabernacling With the Children of God

The whole of the spiritual path eventually comes down to the separation between material sense and spiritual consciousness, between thinking of the power of God as going to do something for human beings on earth, instead of rising to the spiritual kingdom and realizing that we have left the man of earth and are tabernacling with angels, children of God.

That is why there are two of us in each one of us. There is the man of earth, "the natural man,"[9] "the creature,"[10] terms Paul used to describe the human being, and then there is the other part of us, the son of God, the Christ, immortality. In Paul's ministry the whole of the path was getting rid of mortality and putting on immortality, giving up being the man of earth and instead being that man who has his being in Christ, ceasing from being the natural man and attaining spiritual sonship.

If we talk to each other as men and women and keep our conversation on that level we are entirely of this world, but the moment we see what is looking out through the eyes of a person and tabernacle with that, we are communing with the child of God. Then there is an interchange, a going back and forth that is holy because at that level there is no such thing as male and female, rich and poor, high and low. There is only Christhood.

The more we deal with a patient or student humanly, the more we will be enmeshed in the man of earth while at the same time trying to set him free; whereas we must forget him and tabernacle with the spiritual child, realizing the divine nature and qualities of his true being. "Son, thou art ever with me, and all that I have is thine"[11] does not apply to human beings. It applies to that ageless, never born, never dying child of God. When we understand the meaning of the spiritual kingdom and the children of God, we tabernacle with them right here on earth because here is where they are the moment we stop thinking of their corporeality or their physical sense.

Every time we can restrain ourselves from trying to improve human conditions, we are crucifying our own personal sense, and are rising into the higher state of spiritual sonship.

### *Do You Recognize the "Pearl"?*

The more of a do-gooder nature we have, the more we are enmeshed in mortality. That is why eventually we reach the place where we do not have patients come to our office to take up our time. If they come at all we give them five or ten minutes. Students might be given a half hour or an hour. Eventually to the higher and deeper students, we will give two or three hours. But that is not because we are trying to teach them. That is because we are imparting the gift of God, the grace of God, where some evidence of receptivity has become apparent.

The Master called spiritual truth the "pearl of great price."[12] Could we sit very long with a person who did not know that the pearl was of great price, that it was of value? Could we sit very long with a person who was thinking, "Let me use your 'pearl' tonight to go to a ball with. I'll give it back to you tomorrow." or "Let's go to God and get this pain over with so I can get back to my bridge table"?

We do not refuse help to such as these, but we are not going to let them take up our time. The ones who are going to take up our time are those who have come to recognize that this wisdom we have is the pearl. With these, there is no such thing as time any more, nor is there any effort we would ever withhold. All this cannot be explained to beginning students because they have to be fed the "milk." They have to come gradually to wanting the pearl.

Treatments, prayers, and meditations are on the right track when they are not aimed at improving anyone's humanhood, even our own. If we are not thinking of the spiritual kingdom in terms of improving the human sense, if we are not trying to use God power for a material purpose or to change matter, conditions, and amounts, that is the definite sign that we are abiding in the Word and letting the Word abide in us. As long as our vision is on attaining the kingdom of God and God-realization, we are on the right track. If we are trying to demonstrate manna from the sky, healing the crippled man, or human justice, we are on the wrong track.

## God Is Fulfillment

If our prayer, treatment, or meditation has for its goal attaining God-realization, hearing the Word, seeing the Light, obtaining that divine consciousness, we are working in the right way, and this world will begin to take on a wholly different nature.

Suppose we tried to demonstrate coconuts for an empty coconut tree. Would it do any good to take some from one tree to hang on the other? Would it? That is like money being transferred from one person to another person, and then the person thinks he has made a demonstration. That is not a demonstration.

The demonstration is to look at the barren tree and realize "Ah, the kingdom of God is Spirit, Omnipresence, Omnipotence, Omniscience, and all I'm interested in is the kingdom of God." Then we will look up and there will be coconuts there—not out of season, but in their season. Even out of season, if there is a need for them, they will be there because if we have demonstrated the omnipresence of God, we have demonstrated all that God is God to.

If God is fulfillment, when we demonstrate God, we immediately demonstrate fulfillment. The Infinite Way teaches that we have only one demonstration to make and that is the demonstration of the realization of God. If we demonstrate the realization of God, not only our patient or student will find himself fulfilled in the way he may be thinking of but usually in several other ways that he did not even think about.

The difference between a metaphysical approach and a spiritual approach is that in the metaphysical we are dealing with a person and a condition, while in the spiritual we are dealing only with God-realization, and our demonstration is always the realized presence of God. God is fulfillment. In His presence there is liberty and freedom from all discord and all limitation.

We cannot demonstrate God out here in the world; we cannot demonstrate God in a book; we cannot demonstrate God in a temple: we can demonstrate God only within ourselves. Therefore there must be periods of going within for the God-experience because that is the only place we can experience God or the Christ. Meditation, and meditation alone, provides that opportunity. It does not mean that if we are in a falling airplane, we cannot experience God because we could, but it would be mainly because of our having found God within us.

### *Who Are We?*

Among the ancient manuscripts that have been found, verses called "A Hymn of Jesus" were unearthed, telling that when Jesus knew he was about to be betrayed, he called his disciples together to sing a hymn to God. During this hymn, the Master said these words:

> Who I am thou shalt know
> when I depart,
> What now I seem to be that I am not,
> But what I am thou shalt see when thou comest.

There we have the spiritual secret. We are not going to learn that secret in books, nor in living a busy life, but as we meditate and ponder and as the kingdom of God is revealed to us from within, eventually we will hear, "'This is my beloved Son, in whom I am well pleased.'[13] This is the Christ of God." Then we will know who we are, but if we have not developed this inner ability to commune with our own inner being, we will not learn who *I Am*. Therefore, we will not learn our true identity because who I am, thou art; and who thou art, I am, for there is but

One, one son of God, one *I*. Intellectually we cannot learn it; intellectually we cannot believe it; intellectually we cannot demonstrate it. It is only as the inner Grace is released from us that the spiritual revelations are given to us.

What we call meditation, prayer, or treatment really means the ability to go within and to receive impartations of a spiritual nature. Such impartations do not tell us that the fever has decreased, that the lump has become smaller, or that rheumatism has gone. They merely say, *"I* am in the midst of thee." This brings a release.

Without meditation, the Infinite Way would be nothing but another philosophy. To some it would sound good and to some it would sound nonsensical. To both it would be nothing but a philosophy and such it would remain until it is experienced. But it cannot be experienced through the mind. It can be experienced only through the ability to commune within, and then it speaks up and out through us.

### Demonstrate the Source

In metaphysics the demonstration is conditions, amounts, and persons. In mysticism the demonstration is the grace of God, nothing more. Did Moses, Elijah, Isaiah, Jesus, John, or Paul demonstrate anything other than the realization of God?

Wisdom comes only because of the realization of God. Had there been no realization of God, there would have been no spiritual principles revealed because spiritual principles do not come out of the mind. They come out of the Soul, and until we have demonstrated and realized God, we are not going to have spiritual impartations.

Composers recognize that their music is given to them from an inner realm and perhaps even a few may have known that meditation was the way. Not too long ago a well-known musician told me that when he sat down at the organ he first said to himself, "Mind, get out of the way. Mind, get out of the way." Then he would feel a veil lift, and music would come forth. But first he had to get mind out of the way. In other words, his human thought, his human intelligence, and his human capacity had to get out of the way. Then came the flood.

Some painters and sculptors also recognize that the source is beyond the human mind, and they have received their inspiration by first attaining the realization of God, and then their artistic accomplishment flowed forth from that.

God is the source, and we cannot have the effect until we have the source. So there is no use thinking about demonstrating effects. Let us demonstrate the source, the realization of God, and from that all the other things will follow.

*I,* the Father, and *I,* the son, are one, and *I,* the son, must always be in union with *I,* the Father. This is the divine marriage. This is called union with God, oneness with God, at-one-ment with God. It means that *I,* the son, and *I,* the Father, become consciously one through inner meditation and realization. The moment that *I,* the Father, and *I,* the son, are consciously one, the flow begins. If It has to appear as manna, It does; if It has to appear as a publisher, It does; if It has to appear as dollars, marks, or pounds, It does, but not separate and apart from *I,* the son, and *I,* the Father.

The teacher has nothing to teach, nor has the practitioner power to heal, until *I,* the son and *I,* the Father are consciously one, and *I,* the Father, speaks through *I,* the son, or speaks as *I,* the son. But when *I,* the son, and *I,* the Father are consciously one, *I,* the Father, flows through as His rightness of health, His rightness of supply, His rightness of whatever it may be.

## ACROSS THE DESK

What does it mean to live by Grace? Is not Grace God realized as individual consciousness? We have no assurance that we are living under Grace unless God is consciously realized. Although we may have moments of God-contact and feel the joy and security of this realization in meditation, these moments must be continuously renewed many, many times a day by dipping briefly within to let our consciousness of God be released through us into our daily affairs. If this is not done continuously, the pressure of daily living takes over, and we seem to lose the peace and harmony of our periods of meditation.

Living by Grace—the maintaining of our continuous conscious God-contact and the permitting of it to flow out from the kingdom within—results in God-consciousness being expressed as the harmony, peace, joy, and abundance of our daily life.

TAPE RECORDED EXCERPTS
Prepared by the Editor

Omnipresence

"Watch what a realization of omnipresence does to your consciousness. You can let go of thinking; you can let go of taking thought; you can let go of the belief that somewhere God is, and why can't I find Him? Of course you cannot find Him when that 'Him' is you; the 'Him' you are seeking constitutes your very being. God is your mind; God is your life; God is your soul; God is your spirit; and your body is the temple of the living God.

"No reaching out, just relaxing in His word, relaxing in this truth: omnipresence, omnipresence! Where I am, God is. I can never escape out of God, nor can God escape out of me, for we are one. I live and move and have my being in God and God in me: I in Him, and He in me—inseparable, indivisible, omnipresent. There is no fear, then, on a battlefield; and there is no fear in the presence of bombs; and there is no fear in the presence of germs. Why? You are not separate and apart from God: you are in and of God, and God is in and of you.

"The truth of omnipresence lifts us into a state of consciousness whereby we relax mental effort. We relax the strife and the struggle and rest in His word."

Joel S. Goldsmith, "From the Letter of Truth to Consciousness," *The 1961 Laurelton Special Class.*

*Chapter Eight*

# Infinite Way Protective Work

Until this past century the knowledge of the source, cause, and nature of evil and how to free oneself from it was not available to seekers. Heretofore the church had encouraged its people to pray to God to keep them safe while driving on the road or traveling in the air. Such prayers have not been effective, nor have prayers to God for the safety of their children at the front in wartime while they were being shot at or shooting at others. This failure to receive answers to prayers is due to the fact that religious teachings have not understood the nature or the cause of error and the protective work necessary to free oneself from it, all of which is incorporated in the message of the Infinite Way.

There is no use in praying to God to give or to perpetuate our health, our wealth, our safety, or our security. There have been too many good people as well as bad people, religious people as well as irreligious people who have discovered that praying to God for their health does not give it to them unless they find the right doctor and can afford his services.

### The Three O's Are the Assurance of Safety

When we discover and understand the meaning of omnipresence, omniscience, and omnipotence, we will have found the secret of safety and security. Because of omnipresence, can we ever be outside the presence of God? If we go up to heaven, He is there; if we go down to hell, He is there; and if we "walk through the valley of the shadow of death,"[1] He is there. We are never outside the presence of God.

The God that is omnipresent is also omniscient, all-knowing and all-wisdom, and knows our need before we do, making it unnecessary for us to pray for anything. Here where we are—up in an airplane, down in a submarine, or on the battle front—here where we are is omnipresence, and the nature of omnipresence is omniscience, all-knowing and all-wisdom.

Omnipresence which is all-wisdom is omnipotent and all-power, so where we are there is no other power. But the secret of freeing ourselves from the discords of earth and maintaining that freedom involves the conscious recognition of omnipresence, omniscience, and omnipotence. Do we then have to turn to God for healing or for protection? No, for the omnipresence of God is the all-wisdom and the all-power, besides which there is no other power. We cannot need protection from the power of God, and there is no other power.

The moment a person prays to God for anything he is at once acknowledging its absence, and in reality he is acknowledging the absence of God, the absence of the all-knowing wisdom, and the absence of the one and only power there is. Not only that, but he is acknowledging that there is a power from which to be protected or freed.

### Building a Consciousness of One Power

Is not the erroneous basis of most religions the belief in two powers? Is not the basis of any truly metaphysical teaching that of one Power, one God, one Presence? This is the teaching of the Infinite Way, and it permits no exceptions or deviation. We do not in one breath say, "Give me a treatment to protect me from mortal mind," and in the next breath, "No weapon that is formed against me shall prosper." The basis of Infinite Way work is abiding in the realization of One: one presence, God; one wisdom, God; one power, God; *and* no other powers.

This is completely covered and thoroughly explained in *The Infinite Way Letters of 1955*², chapter three, which should constitute a daily text for our study. There is also a chapter in *Man Was Not Born To Cry*³ covering this, and the April and May letters of 1964⁴ *(Realization of Oneness)* devoted entirely to the healing ministry of the Infinite Way, setting forth specific principles that must enter into every treatment we give. But there must be the consciousness of what is contained in this material, and all the *1964 Letters* pound away and hammer at the specific principles so that we may develop the consciousness of the message.

### *Seek Understanding Within*

The intellectual knowledge of the Infinite Way is nothing but a foundation until it is so ingrained in us that automatically when anyone turns to us for help, even without our saying anything, inside we are paying no attention to him because we are not going to try to improve his humanhood. We are not even going to acknowledge a power of evil in his experience to be improved. What we are trying to do is to lift him up to fulfill the words of the Master: "Seek ye first the kingdom of God, and his righteousness; and all these things shall be added unto you."⁵

Just what does it mean to seek the kingdom of God and his righteousness? What is the spiritual idea of health? What is the spiritual form of wealth? What is the spiritual meaning of integrity? What is the spiritual meaning of benevolence? What is the spiritual meaning of "love thy neighbor"[6]? God alone can tell us what He means by health, wealth, love, benevolence, grace, and peace. Who else could tell us what God means?

The human concept of health is very limited because everyone expects that after forty or forty-five his health will begin to deteriorate. The human concept of wealth is also limited because there is a belief that wealth has something to do with money that comes and goes with an economy that fluctuates. But God does not come and go, and the riches of God do not come and go; the health of God does not come and go, and the life of God does not come and go. The love with which God envelops us and in which we are supposed to envelop one another does not come and go either. Where then should a person turn for an understanding of these ideas except within and ask: God, who is my neighbor? What is my neighbor? What is this love that I must bear my neighbor? In what way am I my neighbor's keeper? What is Thy grace? What is Thy health? What is Thy wealth?

### *Invisible Consciousness Is the Source of All Creativity*

When we have this understanding, the things in the outer are the added things. Could we possibly produce an invention in the external realm unless we had first received it in our consciousness? And where would it come from? Where do inventions come from? They come into a person's mind from the Invisible, and then from the mind he can produce them out here in steel, wood, iron, plastic, or anything else.

Where do musical compositions come from? We cannot make them up out of the human brain, can we? Where do we go to find out where musical compositions come from? The only thing we know about any creative work is that it comes from the Invisible. That is as far as we can go in knowing. But when it comes from the Invisible into our mind, can we not write it down on paper or play it on the piano?

Do we need anything out here, then, or do we need the inspiration first and then let it appear? Is not this the reason for meditation? How could an inventor invent if he did not close his eyes and listen? Then suddenly comes the idea and it appears outwardly as the added thing. How could a person compose without meditating? How could he compose without sitting down and becoming silent within himself and waiting for a flow from the Invisible? Could we have music out here separate and apart from consciousness? Therefore, with all our getting, let us get consciousness, and everything else will appear externally.

In the present age as in all past ages, there is a world-wide mesmerism that limits human beings to the mind and body. Mind and body are two levels of the same essence, so we must go beyond the mind until we reach the soul, the spirit, or the consciousness of man. Then we find Infinity. If we delve into a man's mind, we will find both good and evil. But when we find the soul of an individual, regardless of what he thinks he is on the human level, we are tabernacling with the Christ.

## Impersonalizing Good and Evil

Because of the world mesmerism which came about with the belief in two powers, it becomes the responsibility of truth-teachings to reveal to the world that the evils of this world are not personal, that they stem from the impersonal source of good and evil and are ameliorated in proportion as they are recognized to be impersonal. No longer will we pin evil upon a person and then try to get rid of it. Instead, immediately we begin to dissolve it by looking at the person with this realization: "This is no part of you. This is the impersonal hypnotism that personalizes evil."

The greatest healing influence in all the world is: "Be still, and know that I am God."⁷ That is how close God is to us—*I*, our Self. We should be able to rest and relax because *I* in the midst of us is God.

### Conscious Awareness of the True Nature of God Is Needed

Protective work is necessary, but protective work really means protecting oneself from the universal belief in two powers, protecting oneself from the universal belief in the absence of God and the nonsensical belief that God is a God to and for the good. He is not a God to the good and He is not a God to the bad: He is God only to those who know that He is.

The foundation of the Infinite Way is that there is no God on earth among men except in proportion as God is realized. That is why there is sin, disease, death, lack, limitation, and all of man's inhumanity to man. God is God only where God is realized. This does not take away from omnipresence, but it is like having a bank account and not knowing about it. We have either forgotten it or somebody forgot to tell us that he had deposited a certain amount of money in our name. So we do not know about it. Of what avail is our bank account? We could very well starve to death because no bank account will or can save us unless we know it is there and know its value.

The *I* of every individual is God, but if we think of our human self as that *I*, we have limited ourselves to our personal sense of life, years, education, and bank accounts. But when we come to the realization that *I* in the midst of us is God, there is no more limitation. The effect of it is to live as Paul described: "I live; yet not I, but Christ liveth my life."⁸ However, unless we *know* that the Christ is our life, that divine sonship is our relationship to God, and that because of that relationship we are one with the Father and all that the Father has, what good does it do us? That truth was of no value to me until I discovered it, just as it was of no value to the world of Infinite Way students until I passed it on to them.

The awareness of the name of God begins to set us free. Of old the name of God was hidden in such a way that people could not misinterpret it or think that human beings are God. More recently some writers have caused a great deal of mischief by making human beings believe that they are God, with the result that they try to demonstrate It and cannot. It must be understood that a human being is not God but that God constitutes all that we are. Then we are no longer human beings.

### Begin Your Day in
### the Consciousness of the Presence

Of themselves the words we use have no power. Only the consciousness with which the words are clothed brings forth fruitage. It is folly, therefore, to begin our day's work without first meditating sufficiently to attain the conscious realization that we are so clothed in the Spirit that we can almost feel the Robe placed around our shoulders, or be given some other sign to show that we ourselves are not doing the work, but that we are the instruments through which it is being done.

This may require, and often does, two, three, four, five, or six periods a day for the teacher or practitioner to go within until again he has that reassurance, so that his work does not degenerate into just mouthing words, giving quotations, or merely expounding on the most advanced metaphysics or mysticism. A student can read all that in books, and if what is coming out of the teacher's or practitioner's mouth has nothing more than a printed page behind it he is giving nothing more than a printed page.

Unless teachers and practitioners do more teaching in regard to what may be called protective work than they have been doing, most of them are not doing full justice to their students. The real nature of protective work has in a large measure been lost, and it has become little more than orthodoxy under a different name, in other words, a looking to God for protection from evil. That is not protective work. Work of that kind can only get a person into trouble.

Genuine protective work is the conscious realization of omnipresence, omnipotence, omniscience: the omnipresence of one Power, the omnipotence of that one Power, and the omniscience of that one Power, and our consciousness of that Power. It is not a protection by a great power from some little powers called accidents, germs, sins, or temptations. Real protective work is the daily, hourly, quarter-hourly, and minute by minute recognition and constant realization of divine grace as the only Power. It is the ability to realize:

> You, Pilate, in any form, can have no power over me.
> There is only one power, God,
> and that is at the center of my being.
> I walk around with It. Where I am is holy ground.
> If I mount up to heaven; I take that one power
> with me, and if I go to hell, hell becomes heaven
> because that one power is with me.

### Recognize All Negative Powers As Nonpower

From morning to night, and night to morning, individuals are going to be faced consciously, unconsciously, and subconsciously with the belief and fear of two powers, whether it is fear of the power of sickness, lack, sin, economics, or the power of war. In this human life, we cannot live one minute without a suggestion of two powers being offered to us: danger on the road, drunken driving, the power of alcohol, the power of drugs. We cannot live a minute without having presented to us, even by subliminal perception, the belief of two powers, and having suggested to us that we had better watch out for that bad power in some form.

We cannot be said to be spiritually illumined except in proportion to our recognition of all negative powers as nonpower. Having a God that destroys our enemies is not illumination. Having a God that destroys our diseases or overcomes our temptations is not illumination. Illumination is the degree in which we realize that God's omnipotence, meaning the omnipotence of our consciousness, makes null any claim or belief, universal or individual, of a power apart from God. That recognition constitutes illumination.

### Recognize Discord As a Universal Malpractice

Any form of discord is never personal but is a form of universal malpractice. If a person were to say, "You are sick"; "You are dead"; "You are dying"; that is a universal malpractice being expressed through the person. We do not have to protect ourselves from such a person: we have to protect ourselves from the *belief* that there is a selfhood apart from God, an activity, power, or presence apart from God. We protect ourselves from the universal belief, but not from the person who is voicing it, because there is no power in the person. We never have to fear either an individual's malpractice or a collective malpractice.

Occasionally I get letters from students active in the work who report that some member of their family has been taken ill, and they want to know if it is malpractice directed at them because they are in this work. Yes, it is malpractice, but it is not the malpractice of an individual or a group: it is the anti-Christ that makes some of us believe that two times two is five, when it is really four, makes others believe that wealth is in money, or makes still others believe that satisfaction is in sex. That is all malpractice. The truth is that the only wealth is in God; the only health is in God; the only satisfaction is in God. All human forms are beautiful adjuncts.

When students are unwilling to do daily protective work, it is because they fear the other power and shy away from the subject entirely. In some cases it may merely be inertia. We like to think that all our students and patients are truthful when they write telling us that while they want to be well, their main concern is their contact with God, but we know from vast experience this is not so. Their main idea is to get well, to get employed, to get rich, or something of that kind, and if they have to take a little God along with it, they will take it.

To those who are serious students, however, it must be clear that we make the harmony of our day by the degree of illumination we bring into that day and that, at any given moment, we are bringing next year's experience into focus. If today we are doing the protective work that brings to us the realization of omnipresence, omnipotence, and omniscience, a divine grace within us, we are preventing a possible accident next week, next month, or next year. But we are doing that *this* moment.

### ACROSS THE DESK

When a call for help comes to the spiritual practitioner, his first conscious act is to drop both the condition and the patient from his thought as he turns within to the kingdom of God to let the truth that makes free pour forth.

Daily and hourly, each of us, as we perform our tasks, must release ourselves and others from what appears as the human picture: good or bad, a picture which must be recognized as illusion, hypnotism, nothingness.

The inner release that pours out through the practitioner from the source constitutes healing, blessing, harmony, and abundance to those who bring themselves to his consciousness. Each individual who embarks on the Infinite Way of life becomes a spiritual practitioner. From that moment on, integrity demands that he practice the principles revealed by the Infinite Way. The path thus opens before him as a joyous outpouring from the kingdom within, blessing all who touch his consciousness.

## Teaching the Infinite Way
### "Practitioner and Patient"

"An Infinite Way teacher or practitioner should rarely find fault with a student, as if the error were in him. Refraining from finding fault, however, does not prevent correcting whatever needs correcting, but with the correction there must be no sense of the error as being in the person. If a teacher goes on a lecture platform and looks out in the audience, thinking that his function is to correct, reform, or heal somebody, he will never reach anyone. A teacher is there only to voice truth.

"In class, the only way a teacher can impersonalize his teaching is to realize that he is voicing truth, but not directing it at any person. Some students will feel hurt because they may take what the teacher says personally. That is not the teacher's fault. Students have to learn to take these lessons impersonally and know that the teacher is teaching truth, not trying to personalize truth or error."

### The Practitioner Must Have No Judgment
### of Those Who Come to Him

"When students are having periods of frustration, periods of seeming to go backwards, that is the very time when the teacher must give the greatest encouragement, because those are natural periods in a student's development, and they keep coming throughout his spiritual life. Sometimes they come thick and fast, often and furiously. The reason is that in some way or other, the spirit and the flesh are engaging in a battle. The individual, knowing or unknowingly, is not surrendering to the spirit, but is maintaining some sense of self. That is when he needs the greatest amount of help, not criticism, not judgment, not condemnation.

"I have seen some beautiful healings that have come to persons who have been to many practitioners and who write, 'I just cannot take the practitioner's criticism any more, his judgment or his faultfinding. Maybe the fault is with me, but that is what I go to my practitioner to be healed of, not to be reminded of.' That is absolutely right. When students or patients come to us, they come to be healed of their errors, not to be reminded of them as they would be in a 'thou shalt not' teaching. We have many 'thou shalts,' but we do not have too many 'thou shalt nots.'

"When our students and patients come to us, do you not see that we cannot enter into any criticism or judgment of them, knowing that whatever degree of error is manifesting in them is only there through ignorance and, as in our own case, who knows how many years it may take to dispel that ignorance? With some of us it has been a long, drawn-out process; with some few it has been rather quick, depending on previous preparation in other incarnations. Therefore, we must be patient with those who come to us; certainly we must forgive 'seventy times seven'[9]; certainly we must not criticize, judge, or condemn them because of their faults, but rather recognize the source as a universal mesmerism. If anyone wants to withdraw from us, he has that privilege, but then when he wishes to return, he has that privilege, too, because we cast out nobody.

"Probably the greater the sinner, the more he is welcome to us, because where can he go except to those who understand that it is not he who is sinning? It is our function to forgive 'seventy times seven.' We do not excommunicate: we allow those to go who wish to go and permit them to return when they wish to return. There are some who will come to us unwilling to accept what we have, and sometimes these we must ask to go, because we have nothing for them. We cannot compel anyone to do anything; therefore the best thing to do, when a person cannot accept the teaching, is to be about his way, because he may find his solution with some other teacher or teaching."

### Do Not Give Students or Patients Human Advice

"Nowhere in the writings do I tell a student what he must or must not do, or what he must give up. I do not tell him to give up smoking; I do not tell him to give up drinking; I do not tell him to give up adultery; I do not tell him to give up anything in which he may be indulging. I ignore all of that. The fact that he has come to me for help is proof of his desire to be free. I hold him in the truth of his spiritual identity and let the other things dissolve of their nothingness.

"Our goal is to help students to become free, not by repression or suppression, but by spiritual enlightenment. When the Christ touches consciousness, a person will be freed of smoking, drinking, or whatever may be holding him in bondage, and when he is sufficiently touched by the Christ he will be more and more freed of reliance on material means. Infinite Way teachers and practitioners do not set themselves up as judges, telling their students and patients what they should do, because if a person has a broken bone, he cannot walk on his leg without crutches, so what is the use of fooling himself. If the practitioner could rise high enough to give the patient an instantaneous healing so that he could walk and the teacher had the consciousness to say, 'Rise, pick up your bed and walk,' all well and good, but otherwise he should not advise the patient not to use crutches.

"If a patient has diabetes and has to take insulin for the time being, or if he has heart trouble and it is necessary to take digitalis, or if he has some other ailment, let him alone and keep giving him help. The time will come when the teacher or practitioner will know whether the patient is just using truth as a crutch, and then is the time for the practitioner to drop the case and say, 'No, you are not really making the effort to go this way, and I have others who are.' But otherwise, he does not intrude into the student's family or personal life, but tells him to work it out and works with him for his freedom. If that freedom is not attained and the practitioner sees that the student is not really trying hard enough, then he can break away.

"I do not tell patients they must stop taking medicine, because as long as there is some faith in it, taking medicine away from them could create more problems than letting it be a suffer-it-to-be-so-now. What I am interested in is not what the student is doing or thinking when he comes to me but the changes that take place as he continues to come. If I see that changes are taking place in his consciousness, I can be sure that the errors are leaving him.

"Some practitioners have given up cases because it seemed necessary for the patient to take medication or go to a hospital. That is not our concern. Our function is to respond to the calls that come to us, and the only time we dismiss anyone is when there is an evident lack of integrity or when the degree of argumentation is so great that we just cannot continue because we have no time to waste on arguments.

"We do not moralize; we do not psychologize. We pay no attention to bad humanhood and make no attempt to make it good humanhood. We impart spiritual truth and ignore the appearance, not looking for the evil to turn to good because that is not what we are seeking. We are seeking evidence that the Christ has touched an individual. When It does, the Christ will do the work. When we bring the Christ to an individual, It will see to it that his diseases are healed, his sins are washed out, his lack is eliminated. The Christ does that, not you or I; not the Infinite Way—the Christ. Our function is to awaken the individual to the Christ, and this we do by our method of teaching.

"Letters come to me from persons whose practitioners have given up their cases because they had no more money to pay. My personal conviction is that Infinite Way practitioners should not charge specific fees for healing work, but should leave all expressions of gratitude for healing work in the realm of individual demonstration, gratitude, or the ability to pay, and keep the healing ministry clear on that point.

"Specific charges, however, must be made for teaching. If there is not a specific charge for a class, everybody in the city would be in the class, and all they would be doing would be holding back the level of the class because they are not seriously interested in the teaching. There should be fees for teaching in classes and even for teaching individuals until such time as a person grows to that point where he understands the nature of the work. Then there is no use putting any price on teaching because the student has already reached the place where that is not necessary. I have not had any charge for teaching work of an individual nature or with small groups, because in one way or another, students have a way of expressing their gratitude. But when I am giving classes for the general public, there is always a charge, whether it is a one-night, two-night, or a full six-night class."

## Keep Your Relationship With
### Students and Patients on the Spiritual Level

"Spiritual teachers do not get involved in the personal lives of their students because they cannot then be of major help to them. Everyone, as long as he is in the flesh, will have some problems, and if the teacher is to be able to help him with his problems, he must not want to know too much about them, be involved in them, or have opinions about them. The teacher or practitioner should be in the position of not taking sides, giving opinions, or suggesting human footsteps, but responding with 'Good, I will take up work for it.' The teacher is always in the position where he and the student are one, but that oneness is spiritual, not human. Students go to the teacher with questions about their personal lives, and the teacher must be able to answer impersonally, something which cannot be done once the teacher becomes involved in their personal lives.

"In some movements practitioners or teachers take patients into their homes to live with them while they are trying to bring about a healing. Such a practice makes it impossible to maintain that there is nothing to be healed and to look away from the human situation and be present with the Divine. True, somebody must look after patients needing help humanly, but that person should not be the practitioner or the teacher. The one who is looking after them humanly should be someone working with them at that level, while the practitioner maintains his position in spirit.

"The practitioner or teacher is constantly asked such questions as: Shall I take medicine? Shall I discontinue medicine? Shall I advertise for a job or shall I do this or that humanly? The teacher's answer is that none of that is his business. His business is to give spiritual help. He has no authority to tell anyone to stop taking medicine or to interfere in his family life. If there is a husband who wants a doctor for his wife or his children, the practitioner should not interpose or inject his convictions or offer any advice that would antagonize the family or disrupt the family life. If there is a mother who wants shots for her children, the practitioner has no right to have any opinion on the subject.

"No advice should ever be given as to whether or not students should go to a doctor or have an operation. The practitioner should say, 'That is something that has to be resolved within the family. You must keep peace with your family, even if it is a suffer-it-to-be-so-now.' The practitioner must take the attitude that since there is no evil, there can be no evil consequences. There are those in metaphysics who are so superstitious they believe that if they take an aspirin or have an operation

God will punish them, but we who have been in the work have found that some of us wear eyeglasses, others wear earphones, and others arch supports. God has not punished us for that, so it is folly to separate one branch of *materia medica* from another and say, 'Yes, go to a dentist,' or 'Wear eyeglasses, but do not go to other kinds of doctors.'

"The practitioner is called upon only for spiritual help, and that he gives regardless of a person's religious convictions as long as he desires it. The religious convictions of a person can make no difference. Most persons are really atheistic or paganistic anyway, and I do not think there is any one more so than another. Most persons have a God separate and apart that they go to, to have something done for them, without expecting any change on their part. 'God, do this for me. I am going to be the same tomorrow as I am today, but please take my discords away and give me harmony.' It is all nonsense.

"A practitioner is not, however, supposed to answer a call that comes from a neighbor for the neighbor's neighbor down the street who is in need but who has not indicated any desire for help. He does not attempt to help those who do not specifically request help. The only exception to that rule is with young children who would have no knowledge of spiritual help, with the mentally incompetent, or with those who are so sick that they are unconscious. Even then the request for help must come from those closest to the patient.

"When a teacher is asked for help and the spirit of God touches him, students get answers to their problems, and usually in a way that the teacher could not have outlined for them. The teacher or practitioner never lets his thought go to the students' or patients' problems because he does not know in what manner or on what day they should be solved. Much depends on the student's readiness. No outer circumstances can be greater than the degree of illumined consciousness, and therefore, many problems may last a while until that illumination comes.

"The lack of illumination stems from the belief that persons live by externals: by power out here, by money, by investments. Sometimes their problems cannot be met until there wells up within their own consciousness, the truth. 'I live "by every word that proceedeth out of the mouth of God.[10]" In that illumination, their whole life changes in the external."

Joel S. Goldsmith, 1963 *Instructions for Teaching the Infinite Way* and *1963 London Work.*

*Chapter Nine*

# The Simplicity of
# the Healing Truth

The mystical approach to spiritual healing, as practiced in the Infinite Way, cannot be accomplished by anyone until the metaphysical principles of the Infinite Way are so much a part of him that they have become like his flesh and bones. In other words, the mystical consciousness is developed through the metaphysical aspects of the Infinite Way, because in it there are consistent specific principles which develop consciousness.

The Infinite Way does not teach one day that a person's wrong thinking produced his troubles and then the next day teach that his wrong thinking is not the cause. The metaphysical principles of the Infinite Way are completely consistent and are based on the truth that God is infinite consciousness and that man and the universe are this Consciousness formed and expressed.

### *You See Your Concept of a Thing or a Person*

Since God is incorporeal Spirit, man and the universe are incorporeal, and just as you have never seen God with your eyes, and never will, neither have you ever seen man or this universe with your eyes. With your physical sense of sight you have never seen a tree, nor have you ever seen flowers as they are in the consciousness of God. All that you see with your eyes is a finite concept of God's creation built on the universal belief in two powers. That is why you see concepts that are sometimes bad and sometimes good, sometimes young and sometimes old, sometimes sick and sometimes well, sometimes alive and sometimes dead. But these are not creations of God. These are creations of man; they are man-made concepts.

When a student looks at me, he does not see me: he sees a concept he has formed in his mind of me. On the other hand, if I should ask my neighbor to describe me, that student would not recognize me because that is not the *me* he has formed in his mind. If it were possible to speak to my mother, it would still be a different concept of me. None of these has ever seen the real me.

If a student is in meditation and reaches a high enough consciousness, he may then see and know me exactly as I am, but that will be only when he is entertaining no concepts of me and has risen above the mind, beholding me with the vision that God gives him.

### This World, a State of Hypnotism

The basis of Infinite Way metaphysics is that God is consciousness and that this entire universe including man is that Consciousness expressed in Its own image and likeness and formed of the same substance, same quality, same quantity, same nature and same character. From that premise, it follows that all that is true of God is true of man and the universe, but you do not see this with your physical sense of sight.

This world which you do see, however, is a state of hypnotism. To understand that clearly, let me remind you that when an individual is hypnotized he can see, hear, taste, touch, and smell whatever the hypnotist puts into his mind so that he is never aware of anything but hypnotism in different forms.

Let us suppose that in his hypnotized state a person sees a thousand wild beasts coming at him. Are they wild beasts or are they forms of hypnotism? Are they ever really externalized as beasts? If a man in a hypnotized state saw himself burning up in a fire, would there be a fire there and would he be burning up? Would he? No, because the substance of the fire is hypnotism, is it not?

If a millionaire were hypnotized and saw himself in the form of a beggar, would that make him a beggar? Is there a beggar there? Is there anything there but hypnotism? Suppose a poor man is hypnotized and pictures himself as a millionaire. Can he go out and spend his money? No, he hasn't any. He has only hypnotism.

### No Destructive Powers in God's Creation

The healing principle of the Infinite Way is that God is consciousness, universal infinite consciousness, appearing, formed, and expressed as individual man and the universe. This is a spiritual universe, and since every appearance of error is the product of hypnotism—a hypnotism caused by a belief in two powers—there is no such thing as cancer, consumption, poverty, unemployment, an erroneous person, or a sinner. In the proportion that you see such things, you are hypnotized; you are seeing forms of hypnotism. Only when you are de-hypnotized will you see a person as he is. Only then will you see God as God is, and God's universe as it is.

In your purely human state certain germs can cause disease. As a metaphysician, however, not only do you not catch these diseases but because you are de-hypnotized they are healed. Why? Because in your de-hypnotized state, you see these germs in their true light, and know then that they cannot be destructive because God has never introduced anything into His universe to destroy it. Had he done so, how could there be immortality, eternality, or infinity?

### The Cause of All Discord Is Hypnotism

No person engaged in Infinite Way healing work would ever look to a person's wrong thinking as the cause of any erroneous condition he may be experiencing. Whether it is lack, limitation, sin, false appetite, disease, death, war, man's inhumanity to man, or an unhappy marriage, there is only one cause: hypnotism.

The error is in the universal belief in two powers—which is so hypnotic that it makes a person see pictures that are sometimes good and sometimes evil. He is not responsible for that; he did not create this world; and furthermore he has never created any of the troubles that he has ever had in his life. In every case he has been the victim of a universal belief in two powers, a belief which is so hypnotic that he has come under it. In his hypnotized state, he believes that a certain person has done him an injustice. But if there is only one power, is there any power of injustice? So before he could even see and then condemn that person he would have to be hypnotized by a belief in two powers.

### To Be Convinced That the Appearance
### Is Hypnotism Is To Be Free

In the Infinite Way there is one cause of all discords: hypnotism. When you are convinced of this, that is the end of your treatment because you do not do anything to hypnotism. After you have recognized the cause as hypnotism, there is nothing more for you to do.

Do you not see that when a person can recognize hypnotism he is no longer hypnotized? If you were to tell a hypnotized person that what he is seeing is not there, however, you could not convince him of it because he is in a hypnotized state. Conversely, when a person is de-hypnotized, you could not convince him that he had ever believed it. That is why, first of all, your treatment consists of knowing that the consciousness which you are is the cause of this entire creation, including everyone in it, and that any appearance of materiality—even a good one—is a state of hypnotism, and that is why you do not work to get rid of the flames, the cancer, or the unemployment because if you got rid of them you would still be hypnotized, and hypnotism would then take another form.

What you have to do is to lay the axe at the root, and when you are convinced that the root is hypnotism, you are free, and the person you are helping is free. If it does not happen on the first realization, it may be that your realization has not been sufficiently deep. Then, too, there may be a thousand reasons why patients still cling to their problems and personalize them. The point is that you are responsible only for you. You have to decide whether or not the Infinite Way registers with you, whether or not this is the truth for you.

If you insult your own intelligence, you cannot succeed. Making affirmations about something you *hope* to become, walking around affirming, "I am the child of God! I am the child of God!" while all the time you are suffering, or continuously repeating, "I am rich; I am the son of God," and you are not, is insulting your own intelligence.

There is no faith healing about this work. The work of the Infinite Way is knowing the truth, and the truth has to do with the truth of creation, the nature of God, man, and the universe. The nature of God is Consciousness, which I am. The nature of the universe and man is infinite, spiritual consciousness, forming Itself as you and as me, as the trees, the birds, and the beasts.

What of this world? It is a world of appearance, based on the Adam-and-Eve belief in two powers—good and evil—which has become so hypnotic that everyone sees almost identical hypnotic pictures. The world finds a cure for one incurable disease and then finds another incurable disease. It gets rid of one, and a new one suddenly makes its appearance.

The day must come when you stop playing around with coughs, colds, flu, heart disease, tuberculosis, and cancer and begin to recognize that this whole world is but a form of hypnotism presenting itself as a world condition or as a sick person, a poor person, or an unemployed person. Always, however, it is a state of hypnotism.

## Come Out and Be Separate

Unless you can keep yourself separate from the world, you, yourself, will be a part of this world hypnotism. You cannot permit yourself to indulge in world-hypnotism and at the same time claim it is not there. The day will come when you will decide to live your life separate and apart from people, except that you go among them to reveal this truth, but not to live in their lives. When you begin living the lives of your family, your friends, and the people of this world, you are accepting their hypnotism at its face value. That is as nonsensical as the practitioners who set aside two or three hours a day to handle their practice or to go to an office and be a practitioner. What are they doing the other twenty hours in the day? Do they think that going to an office for four hours can possibly make them practitioners?

You have to live this Infinite Way of life out in the world. The only way you can live it is to be in it to the extent of revealing truth but not to the extent of trying to live the lives of other persons for them, because the lives that are being led out here are a hypnotic experience, an unreal experience, based on the whole belief of good and evil.

While there are some who believe that there must come a stop to being philanthropic, because there really is nobody to be helped, and therefore philanthropy is merely indulging in another form of world hypnotism, I do not advocate this at the present time. I advocate taking into consideration that there are degrees of consciousness, and that if somebody asks for bread, do not give him a stone. If you can help him, do it without accepting his state as a real one, knowing that you are helping him only at his level of consciousness.

### No Amounts in Spirit

Until Infinite Way students arrive at the place where these two major unfoldments—the nature of the spiritual universe as consciousness formed and the nature of this world as hypnotism—constitute their understanding of this message, they cannot succeed because, according to the Infinite Way, all there is to spiritual healing is knowing the nature of God and the nature of error as a state of hypnotism. It is not trying to correct a state of error, not trying to improve it, not trying to reduce a fever from 104° to 101°, and then to 98.6°, but to recognize that all temperatures are a part of the material dream. In Spirit there are no temperatures, not even normal temperatures. There is no blood pressure in Spirit; there are no heartbeats in Spirit. You are not concerned with changing the nature of a person's health because in God there is no health: only eternality. Nothing ever disturbs eternality. "I and my Father are one,"[1] therefore, *I* am eternal, *I* am infinite.

There are no amounts of supply. When you count the blades of grass in the lawn or the leaves on a tree, you will soon discover that there is no such thing as a large amount or a small amount: there is only infinity. If it were all burned up in one day, the next day it would be right there growing again, because there is only infinity, nothing less.

The number of dollars in your possession today does not represent your supply. If you spent them, gave them away, burned them up, or inflation destroyed them, in the very next second they would begin to multiply again. Infinity is forever flowing. You cannot stop the flow of infinity as long as you recognize God as infinite consciousness expressing Itself.

God cannot stop expressing Itself on a certain date any more than He can begin expressing Himself this minute, or after you have given a treatment. The patient is not really any better after you have given a treatment than he was before. It is only that now he is exhibiting more of his divine Selfhood. You do not make him better than he was through your treatment: you merely bring out a greater measure of his divinity.

Unless you know God aright, you might just as well stop praying. But if you understand God to be the infinite consciousness of this universe, which means that It must be the consciousness of you and me, then you can pray, and your prayer is a communion with your inner Self. It is not a seeking of anything: it is merely an acknowledgment of the infinite nature of your own consciousness appearing as infinite, harmonious form.

### *The Substance of "This World"*

If I am one with the Father, I must be all that God is and must have all that God has. That is basic truth. Against that there is this world. Once you have seen that the basis of this human sense of world is hypnotism, then you can use the analogy of paper as the basic substance. If you make a cat or a dog and a man out of paper, you still have nothing but paper. What is the quality of the cat, the dog, and the man? The quality of paper. How eternal is the life of the cat, the dog, and the man? As eternal as the life of the paper. When there is no longer paper, there is no longer cat, dog, or man, but as long as there is paper, there is cat, dog, or man.

In reality, God is the substance of all form. The nature and character of all form—cat, dog, man, tree, bird, or beast—is God. Therefore they are eternal. But the substance of this world is hypnotism, and you cannot get rid of the errors or the limitations of this world until you get rid of the hypnotism.

When you were rid of the paper, you were rid of the cat, dog, and man. When you are rid of hypnotism, you are rid of sin, disease, death, and all forms of limitation. How do you get rid of hypnotism? By recognizing it. That is the only way.

If somebody presents to you the picture of a sick or sinning mortal man, a sick cat, dog, bird, or beast, and you can say to yourself, "Bosh! Hypnotism!" and mean it, the picture disappears, and you receive a call, "Oh, that was wonderful." What was wonderful? Did you heal the man or animal of anything? Did you have a gift from God that enabled you to do something for him? No, you knew the truth. Knowing the truth means knowing the nature of God and His creation which is "My kingdom,"[2] and knowing the nature of "this world"[2] which is hypnotism.

The longer you work with this truth, the greater the miracles that will happen in your life. At first you accept truth intellectually. You feel it must be right; you work with it; and you begin to get results. Those results are not really miracles but they are enough to show you that you are on the right track. As you continue to work, your consciousness changes from a state of hypnotized consciousness to one of de-hypnotization, and all of a sudden you say, " 'Whereas I was blind, now I see.'[3] This is the kingdom of God." You do not have to go any place to get the kingdom of God; you do not have to die to get there. This is the kingdom of God, and this hell has become heaven. But that is only when you are awakened out of the state of hypnotism.

### Recognize Every Claim
### As a Lie About the Truth

A most important point to remember is that you do not get rid of hypnotism any more than you get rid of rheumatism. You do not overcome hypnotism; you do not struggle with it; you

do not look for a God-power to do something to it. You merely recognize that the substance or the fabric of this world is hypnotism and then drop it.

If you were to see 2 x 2 = 5 on a paper or blackboard, you
would not struggle to overcome it. You would merely say 2 x 2
= 4 and that is that. Or, you might say, "That's a mistake." But
you would not do anything after you recognize it as a mistake
because there is nothing to be done. Once you know it is a mistake it does not fool you any more.

If somebody tells you a lie and you think it is the truth, you
can get into trouble. But if someone tells you a lie and you know
it is a lie, do you have to do anything? You don't even have to
correct the liar, do you? Because you don't care what he is doing.
That is his business. All you have to know is, "That's a lie. I can't
be fooled." Right?

If then a claim of any nature is presented to you and you
recognize, "That is neither person, place, nor thing. That is a
state of hypnotism," that's all you have to do. You are not fooled
by it. You recognize it as a lie, and it has lost its power. Because
there is only one consciousness, the one who has come to you
for help has united himself with you and wakes up and recognizes that it was a lie.

The healing truth is not complicated. It consists of two parts:
knowing God and His creation and knowing the nature of error
and its creation. But attaining the actual awareness that this is true
is the difficult part. What you struggle with is yourself until you
can reach a state of consciousness that can recognize a lie. When
you reach a state of consciousness that does not become fright-
ened at the words, atomic bomb, cancer, tuberculosis, polio,
mongoloid babies, paralysis, blindness, deafness, and can say,
"Oh, that's a lie," then you are in the healing consciousness.

As long as these names or appearances continue to make
you want to do something, you are hypnotized. Do you not see
that the whole of the spiritual path is an internal struggle, tak-

ing place within your own consciousness, not a struggle with what is wrong with the world. There is nothing wrong with the world. What is wrong is your concept of the world. How are you beholding the world? Are you seeing Jesus as a resurrected Hebrew prophet or are you seeing Jesus as the Christ as Peter saw him? Are you seeing man as a mortal, or are you recognizing the Christ incarnate. Do you see the difference? It is as simple as this, and it is as difficult as this. The simplicity is that there are only two important parts: the nature of God and His creation; the nature of error and its creation. That is all. You build your entire spiritual life on those two points.

### The Infinite Ways As Which Hypnotism Appears

An important point to remember is that error can appear in as infinite a number of forms as God's grace can appear. You could never believe all the different forms of error that come to the desk of a busy practitioner: one problem is marital discord, the next parental discord, the next financial discord, the next physical, the next one moral, the next relationships, the next business, the next one unemployment, and the next one age. In addition to all that, you might have actors who want better parts coming to you and musicians who want engagements.

If you were going to treat all these problems, you would not only have to be an M.D., you would have to be a psychiatrist, an adviser on morals, a financial counselor, and a marriage counselor. What comes to a practitioner in the mail and over the telephone is unbelievable and incredible. But you have to remember that none of it is true. Only one thing is true; only one thing comes through the mail and over the telephone: a state of hypnotism, a state of hypnotism appearing in infinite form and variety. That is all.

Infinite Way practitioners are not employment agencies,

marriage counselors, psychologists, nor are they ministers who reform sinners and save souls. Infinite Way practitioners are those who have received the revelation of the nature of God and the nature of error.

If you see a whole city burning, do not run for water to put out the flames. Recognize it as hypnotism. If you see a tidal wave on the way to wipe out a city, do not run around looking for barriers to keep it out. Stand still and recognize it as a state of hypnotism. If you hear of infection or contagion, recognize that, too, as a state of hypnotism. Then watch what happens to the hypnotic picture.

### The Unchanging Nature of God's Abundance

All this is what makes it so difficult for most metaphysicians to understand the Infinite Way. They are approaching it from their metaphysical background and that is not the Infinite Way at all, as you can see. It is difficult, also, for people to understand because of the centuries of orthodox beliefs that are behind them. They cannot catch the vision that God cannot do anything about a situation. They forget that God is the same yesterday, today, and forever, that nothing changes in God, that He cannot inaugurate peace on earth today, tomorrow, or next week, and that in His kingdom there has never been anything but peace. They cannot understand that God cannot heal a disease, nor can they understand that because God never permitted a disease, there never has been a disease to heal.

All that God has been from the beginning, God is now. You may come into the awareness of the harmony of God today, tomorrow, next week, in this lifetime or the next, but the truth is that harmony has always been. You may come into a state of prosperity today which you never knew before, but that prosperity has always been there.

In periods of depression, there is no less gold in the world, no less silver, platinum, diamonds, pearls, potatoes, carrots, meat, wine, or water. In days of poverty, there is no less real wealth in the world than in days of abundance. All that has happened is that in times of prosperity you have come into the awareness and demonstration of it. Even in the depths of the depression of the 1930's, many people became millionaires; many made fabulous fortunes. There was just as much wealth in the world in the 1930's as there is today. How then could a person go to God for wealth? If a person were not getting it, it was not God's fault. His wealth was here, is here, and always will be here. He may not have tuned in, and the reason is that he may have allowed himself to be hypnotized by appearances.

### Recognize Every Appearance As Hypnotism

Looking out in the distance you see the horizon. Can you get rid of it? No, it will never go away because it is not there at all. But even though the appearance remains there, you are not fooled or limited by it. You can go anywhere you want to go on a ship, because you have recognized the horizon for what it is—an appearance. What happens to the mirage on the desert the moment you recognize it as a mirage? It is no longer a condition: it is then just an illusion. You are not disturbed by an illusion, and it does not stop your progress across the desert.

So it is that you do not get rid of evil. An understanding Infinite Way practitioner recognizes every appearance, everything that you can see, hear, taste, touch, and smell, as the product of universal hypnotism. He does not overcome, destroy, or get rid of evil. He drops it. That is the secret of Infinite Way healing work. That is why my work as a Christian Science practitioner flourished for sixteen years and why later in the seventeen years of more of the Infinite Way it continues to flourish and has become known and established throughout the world.

And what established the Infinite Way? One thing and one thing only—the fruitage. There are some Infinite Way practitioners who have a very small practice which does not increase much or very rapidly. There are others who flourish. What is the difference? Those who flourish know the principles exactly, thoroughly, concretely, and work specifically with them. They do not deviate from them or fluctuate back and forth. They do not sympathize; they do not pity. Yet they have enough human understanding to know that in their ignorance they were the same as the rest of the world, so they have never lost the compassion that realizes that as long as persons are hypnotized they are going to know and experience good and evil.

Successful practitioners stand on the two basic principles: the nature of God and *My* kingdom, and the nature of evil and its world of illusion. They stand fast in those principles until they develop the consciousness that is not fooled by appearances.

You cannot rejoice over good health, because even a person with good health can drop dead tomorrow. The only good health that you must attain is the health that comes through the realization of your identity as *I Am*, and from the truth that this world is a hypnotic experience. Then drop it. Do not be concerned with it. Do not fight it. Why do you think the Master taught, "Resist not evil"[4]? Would he have taught that, if you were supposed to fight error? "Resist not evil.[4]. . . Put up again thy sword into his place: for all they that take the sword shall perish with the sword."[5] Those who live by fighting evil will die by that evil.

Once you enter the kingdom of God and realize a spiritual peace, you will at the same time realize that you never had an enemy in any form. All you were faced with was a hypnotic world, the substance of which was hypnotism, and temporarily you were fooled by the pictures formed by that hypnotism. One day it was a fire, one day a tidal wave, the next day a volcano, the next day an epidemic, next day unhappiness, and the next day poverty. Every day hypnotism formed a new picture for you, and as fast as you were able to get out of one picture it produced another picture.

### Letting God's Infinity Express Through You

Lay the axe at the root and say, "You'll not fool me again. I know that the fabric of this world is nothingness, hypnotism. There is no law to any of its pictures: no law of disease, no law of health. The only law is *I Am*, for *I* am the law. There is no law operating in me, on me, or through me, for *I* myself am the law. No good can come to me for *I Am* is the only good. No peace can come to me. *My peace* give I unto you who do not know this truth. But nobody has any peace to give me; nobody has any prosperity to give me; nobody has any health to give me; nobody has any love to give me. *I* am love."

You who are waiting to be loved are going to wait seven thousand years and more because the only love there is, is the love you express. The moment you express love it comes back to you. The bread that you cast upon the water is earmarked to return to you. Love cannot come into your life until you love. Then when it comes into your life it may not come through those from whom you expect or want it to come. No, you have to give up expecting and wanting. If you expect love, you may have to wait an eternity for it to come.

If you want love, you must love. If you want abundance, you must give. If you want companionship, you must be a companion. If you want friendship, you must be a friend. Why? Because you and your Father are one, and you already have all that the Father has.

In this letter the simplicity of the Infinite Way is revealed, but you also see that the difficulty is going to be when you begin to practice it. Then it is a matter of self-discipline. You cannot indulge yourself in worldly things and expect to practice this. You have to keep yourself separate from the world so that nothing destroys your awareness.

### Across the Desk

Because of the many misconceptions of what love really is, the book *The Gift of Love*[6] will do much to dispel some of these false concepts and reveal its real meaning. Although *The Gift of Love* is especially designed for those, with or without a metaphysical background, seeking an answer to the meaning of love, nevertheless it will become a manual for serious Infinite Way students who seek to make love a way of life.

### Tape Recorded Excerpts
#### Prepared by the Editor

#### Omnipresence

"Only those are in lack who are not living in the constant acknowledgment of the omnipresence of God. Even very religious people can be in lack and limitation because they never acknowledge God in the midst of *them*. It is always God maybe in the midst of a priest, a rabbi, a minister, or a practitioner, but they never acknowledge God in the presence of themselves. Sadly enough, the more religious people seem to be, the more they are acknowledging God in someone else and are afraid to acknowledge It in themselves, as if it were something unholy to acknowledge It in themselves, as if it were something unholy to acknowledge, 'God in the midst of me.' And yet what is the entire teaching of Christ Jesus? . . . God is in the midst of you— and he did not say all you saints: he just said 'you.'

"Acknowledge Him in all thy ways. Acknowledge the presence of God in your consciousness. Acknowledge the presence of God in your soul, in your mind, in your body. Acknowledge the presence of God in your business. Acknowledge the presence of God in your art, in your writing, or whatever your work may be. Acknowledge that God is the source."

Joel S. Goldsmith, "Between Two Worlds," *The 1964 Portland Special Class.*

"You are not confined to your body. Then, are you dangling around in space here over your head? No, you are omnipresence: *I* am omnipresence. *I* am here, and *I* am there, and *I* am everywhere. 'The place whereon thou standest is holy ground,' for *I* am there. *I* am omnipresence. . . . I know that *I* am not born and *I* will not die for I am that I Am. . . . I am equally at home in any part of the world because *I* am throughout the world. *I* embrace this world in my consciousness. . . . I am in you, and you are in me, and we are in God, for we are all one; we are the *I Am.* . . . We are all in and of one Presence, Omnipresence."

Joel S. Goldsmith, "I Am," *The 1962 Chicago Closed Class.*

"You know now that you are omnipresence. Ah, but before this, do you know what you said? God is omnipresence. Well, now, what were you? Ah, there it is again: we have a God and a you. Now you will know *I* am omnipresence, and therefore, *I* am where you are wherever you are. Out in the ocean in a boat, lost in the desert, *I* am there: *I* am where you are."

Joel S. Goldsmith, "The Pearl," *The 1962 Chicago Closed Class.*

# Chapter Ten

# Educating the Human Mind Out of Itself

Aspiritual teaching can never be known or taught through or by the human mind. Only a person who has attained some measure of that mind that was in Christ Jesus, the ability to discern spiritually, can teach spiritually. Then his teaching ultimates in lifting up the consciousness of the individual, raising up the son of God, and developing spiritual discernment in the student.

If a person had all the knowledge of truth that is in all the Infinite Way books, he would still find himself without spiritual power, unless in the study or reading of the books his spiritual discernment had been developed. Since spiritual truth is the very opposite of what might be called common sense or intelligence in the human world, obviously, imparting spiritual wisdom is difficult and, if not clearly understood, impossible.

The first thing that must be understood is what a teacher is trying to accomplish. And what is he trying to accomplish but to educate the human mind out of itself?

### *Good and Evil, Determined by Our Conditioning*

The human mind is made up of certain laws, theories,

and convictions that have been inherent in it for generations, and which are inherited at birth. One of these is the belief in good and evil. The human mind is convinced of the existence of good and evil and decides for itself what is good and what is evil. Interestingly enough, what is good in one place may be evil in another place. What is evil in one place may be good in another.

Furthermore, what is evil to one person can be good to another. You may have a beautiful garden of roses which to you is magnificent, God's perfect expression, but another person may become ill with rose fever from being in that garden with the roses. To some persons, animals, cats, and dogs may be the most loving creatures of God, but another person is made miserable and sneezes all day and all night after being in their presence. To one, the dog or the cat becomes evil, and to another, it is good. To one, roses are magnificent, and to the other, they are to be avoided.

You can sum up what in your society is called good and what is called evil, and then look at some other societies in the world and see if there is agreement on what is good and what is evil. Eventually the realization must come that nothing is good or evil except for a person's attitude toward it, his acceptance or reaction to it. You and I probably would never want to go inside a lion's cage, and yet lion tamers go there seemingly without any fear. There are some persons who have collections of reptiles, and they are at home with them, even though no one else would dare to go near them because they still have their poisonous fangs.

You might rehearse for an hour or two those things that you have automatically accepted as good and as evil. Does it not all depend on a person's reaction, where he was born, and how he was brought up? There are persons fearing an invisible satan; there are persons fearing a church; there are persons fearing some particular ethnic group.

### *The Spiritual Teacher Must Have Attained a State of Nonreaction to Appearances*

How many things there are in our society that we judge morally bad which others feel are not bad at all! The spiritual teacher must have attained the consciousness that there is nothing out here either good or evil, in and of itself, regardless of appearances. It is the reaction to it that makes it good or evil. When a person seeks help for an illness of one kind or another, the human mind usually responds with "Ah, this is evil," and must quickly procure certain medication. The spiritual practitioner, however, must already have risen to the state of consciousness which recognizes that nothing is evil and that only a reaction or belief in it makes it so.

When a spiritual teacher has arrived at that consciousness, then the teacher's work is to bring the student to that same state of spiritual consciousness. This means not merely imparting the letter of truth, but lifting the student in consciousness to where he, too, can sit down in the presence of the "lion" and know that the lamb and the lion can lie down together, because they are both of the nature of God. Students may not have to face actual lambs and lions, but many times the principle is proved between husbands and wives, where the husband is a lion and the wife a lamb or vice versa, and where harmonious living together is realized in experience.

The human mind is a belief in two powers. Only as the spiritual teacher can, through precept and example, lead and educate the student out of his belief in two powers, does the human mind of the student relax and release itself and become receptive to the things of God.

One characteristic of the human mind is to sit in judgment. No one can expect to attain Christ-consciousness until the human mind has relinquished all criticism, condemnation, and judgment. As long as the mind retains the desire, the will, or the wish to judge, it remains the human mind, unreceptive to the things of God. But when the human mind can ask, "Father, reveal the nature of this appearance," then it is not sitting in judgment. It is not calling one thing good and another evil, one moral and one immoral, one honest and one dishonest, one free and one slave. Eventually there must be a complete relinquishment of all judgment. "Who made me a judge or a divider over you?[1] . . . Neither do I condemn thee"[2]—neither do I hold thee in bondage to any sense of right or wrong.

What happens when even a measure of this takes place in consciousness? What happens when so much of the human mind begins to disappear that you are constantly looking out and enjoying *is* and not judging by appearances? Whatever it is that you are looking at, you are not labeling it good, nor are you labeling it evil. What you are doing is realizing *is*. What it is you may not know, but you do know that it is, and then you let the Father reveal to you who or what it is. In the end spiritual discernment will say, "Knowest thou not, this is My beloved son?" But it will not only say that of Jesus the Christ, it will say that of the identity of every individual and of the partially attained son of God in every seeker who is honestly seeking and knows what he is seeking.

### Only in an Illumined Consciousness Does Evil Not Exist

The student who is just beginning has no way of knowing what he is seeking. Even if he has read or been told what he should be seeking he probably would be unable to recognize it, because it would make no sense to him. Only the teacher and the student who are on the path, even though they have not yet attained, recognize what they are seeking and know how much further they have to go. With Paul they will admit, "'Not as though I had already attained,'[3] but at least I do know that, as far as I am concerned, I must relinquish the belief in two powers. Just as I must relinquish a good and evil anything, so I must relinquish a good power and an evil power. If not, I will be making the mistake of so many churches and be seeking a God-power to do something to evil. They have never succeeded. There is no God-power to do anything to evil because in the presence of God-power there is no evil."

In the three-dimensional mind, the human mind, there is a great deal of good and evil, just as there is light in the day and darkness at night. Only in the presence of illumined consciousness is evil not evil. No one can correctly claim that disease, sin, or false appetite has no power when the whole world is suffering from these appearances. But in the presence of the illumined or Christ-consciousness evil does not exist.

As we consider the idea of neither good nor evil, it is not enough to realize, "There is fulfillment." Let us always remember to add the words, "in Thy presence." In Thy presence, there is fulfillment. In the presence of whatever state of illumination you have attained is fulfillment, not because of you, but because of the state of consciousness that realizes one power and that there is neither good nor evil out here in effect.

### Self-Preservation, the Essence of the Human Mind

The last stand of the human mind, its last ditch fight, is self-preservation, the law that would compel you to save your life at someone else's expense, the law that would say, "Let us drop the bomb first because it will save our lives," or the law that, even though legal, permits a person to shoot a burglar in his home. Consciousness would say, "No, no!" Illumined consciousness does not hold the burglar's life as less valuable than your property or as less valuable than your life, because just as the Magdalene became one of the greatest of the followers of the Christ, how do you know but what that burglar may some day become another Christ? Therefore, you cannot sit in judgment and say, "Your life is worthless in comparison to mine."

It is not you and I who believe in the law of self-preservation: it is the human mind, the carnal mind, which is built up
on the word "I." I, me, and mine constitute the human world,
that false sense of I which will do anything for "me or for mine."
As you relinquish this idea of self-preservation, you broaden
your horizon and while providing for the support of your family, you also begin to contribute to some other family that temporarily may not have enough.

Consideration of others is "love thy neighbor as thyself"⁴ in
action. Loving thy neighbor as if thy neighbor were thyself, you
will see that you are not functioning from the level of the
human mind because the human mind would never feel that
way. The human mind is interested only in "me," "my children," and "my country." That is the human mind. But to "love
thy neighbor as thyself" and to pray for your enemies is the
Christ-mind.

These are aspects of the human mind out of which every
student must be educated in some measure before there is
enough of the Christ-mind to enable him to receive and to
understand the things of God. In working with the letter of
truth, the spiritual teacher must not only understand these
aspects of the human mind from which the student must be set
free, but the teacher must himself have been educated out of
those phases of the human mind so that he can look out without judgment.

To teach without judgment does not mean without the ability to correct, because always, as you are presented with the
human mind, you see its aspects which must be corrected in the
student. Such correction is not sitting in judgment on the student, condemning, blaming, or holding him responsible for
some failure; but is understanding that each one is presenting
aspects of the human mind and that the function of a teacher is
to point these out and attempt to bring about ways of correct-

ing them. So the teacher, then, brings out these aspects of the human mind and all the illustrations that will help to dissolve the human mind.

## The Real Reason for Benevolence

It is generally believed that our charity and benevolence are for the sake of the poor, the downtrodden, and for those who do not have. That has made it very difficult for a sufficient amount of charity and benevolence to go forth into the world, because it is hard to make a person come to the conclusion that he really should give up so much of his own possessions even for the poor and the downtrodden. The human mind persists in clinging to itself and its own. But giving to the poor or the have-nots has nothing to do with being charitable or benevolent.

The real reason for benevolence and charity is found in Jesus' statement, "Inasmuch as ye have done it unto one of the least of these my brethren, ye have done it unto me."[5] In other words, you are my Self, and I am your Self, and there is no such thing as your Self separate from my Self. The Self of me is God; the Self of you is God; and since there cannot be two Gods, the same God that is the Self of me is the Self of you. Therefore, whatever I do unto you I am doing unto my Self—not unto you, and not for you, not out of pity for you, and not out of love for you, but out of love for my Self, the one Christ-Self, God.

At one time a committee seeking to build a hospital in a small town where there were inadequate hospital facilities wrote to me. Their problem was to raise a million and a half dollars which to the human mind would present a problem. My answer was that whatever they believed they were trying to do for sick, poor, or crippled people, they were doing unto the Christ. Therefore, this activity in which they were engaged must be an activity of the Christ because its object is to serve "the least of these my brethren."

The responsibility of paying for this hospital was not theirs. They were the messengers, the transparencies, serving the Christ, because on the human level of life, hospitals, mental institutions, homes for the aged, and nursing homes are necessary, and since they are a service to the poor, the sick, and the needy, they are a service unto the Christ.

There may come a day when human consciousness is so completely evangelized that there will be no sickness to heal or poverty to eliminate. Then the Christ-activity will be of an entirely different nature. But just as Infinite Way practitioners are doing spiritual healing, which is a recognition of the fact that there are those under the belief of sin, sickness, and lack, and are serving through spiritual means, so those seeking to build hospitals are doing the same thing through the highest means at their command. Their desire to build a modern and complete hospital is as Christ-like as the desire to bring forth harmony through spiritual means.

You must embody the principle of one Self and must learn that the one Self appears as infinite form. Just as you would feed yourself three times a day, educate yourself, clothe yourself, or house yourself, you must do this for your Self in many forms. All are not awakened to their Self, to their true identity. As long as they are in ignorance of their Self, they will be poor, and at some period they will need help of one kind or another. But when you give help, you must always remember that you are doing it unto your Self in many forms.

### The Ancient Method of Giving the Higher Teaching

The principle of inasmuch-as-ye-have-done-it-unto-one-of-the-least is stated over and over again in the writings, but reading about it is not attaining the consciousness that the I-am-thy-Self-and-thou-art-my-Self is a principle to be worked with.

In seeking spiritual enlightenment Infinite Way students rely principally on the reading of Infinite Way books, attending classes, and hearing the tape recordings. Leading a student to enlightenment through these means is a necessary step, but out of all the students who are studying in this manner, there will be found those who seek to go higher, searching for greater light and striving for greater spiritual attainment. Then is when they may be led to another phase of teaching, one that comes down from the most ancient of days when there were wisdom schools. The manner of teaching in them was to give the student a principle to practice and live with until realization dawned, so that he might realize, "On this point, at least, 'whereas I was blind, now I see.'"[6]

Students often are given the statement: "Thy grace is my sufficiency in all things, and there is a sufficiency of Thy grace omnipresent for the need of this moment." It must be recognized that this spiritual principle is not true in the human picture, because to the human being God's grace is not a sufficiency, nor is there a sufficiency of It present. It is only to the illumined consciousness that that Grace is sufficient and that there is a sufficiency omnipresent.

In the higher teaching, the teacher gives this principle to the student, and the student must live with it and practice it, until some measure of fruitage is evident from abiding with that principle. The measure of fruitage is the measure in which the degree of humanhood has been lost, a humanhood that needed something other than Grace or that felt that there was not a sufficiency at hand.

The teacher works with these principles, not expecting to impart them to a student in a week, two, three, or four, but presenting one principle for a week or two, then another principle for a week or two, and then both principles for a week or two, remembering always that everything comes to fruition in silence and secrecy.

In spiritual teaching as carried on in ancient days, nobody went through a period of training in a week or two. Usually it took seven years, and often seven years of living right in the household or in a building with the teacher. In teaching it is vitally important that not only the words of the teacher, but the consciousness of the teacher, are being imparted and absorbed. While conditions today do not lend themselves to living for years in the home of a teacher, the depth of such teaching could still go on with those students who were sufficiently dedicated as to be willing to take a principle, live with it, and work with it until they embody it.

### Rising Above Words and Thoughts

It is said in the writings that eventually you must come to the place of rising above words and thoughts, above the human mind. You are at the stage where that must be accomplished now, not ultimately. It does not mean that everyone who reads these writings will accomplish it or even want to. It means that for those with whom these statements register, the time has come to rise above the human mind and reach that realm beyond words and thoughts.

Is it not clear that words and thoughts are meaningless unless they can be embodied as consciousness? Therefore, words will be used, not with the idea that there is any power in them, but only as reminders to aid you in rising above them to the consciousness of them.

As an example of the powerlessness of words and thoughts, let us take a situation that seems absolutely impossible of solution: a call from a husband or wife of intolerable living conditions between them and differences that cannot be surmounted. When the appeal comes to you for help, the first thought that inevitably enters your mind is: How can I enter somebody else's household and tell the members of that household what is right

or wrong? And if I could, would whoever is wrong have the ability to give it up? No, it would be impossible. They are too convinced of their rightness, and nothing that you could think or
do of a human nature would be of any value. Therefore, you get
at peace and see what is revealed to you from within. Probably
a thought might come such as, "It is God's grace that meets
every need, and there is a sufficiency of God's grace. Very well,
then, I will be still and listen."

You are convinced that words and thoughts are of no
power; you are convinced that no activity of the human mind
is going to solve this problem, so now you can listen, if only
for ten, twenty, or thirty seconds. You might have to do this
two, three, or four times in the day; you might have to do it
tomorrow and the day after as worse reports reach you. But
nothing can change the fact that God's grace is the sufficiency
and that there is a sufficiency of God's grace now. There cannot, then, be anything further to do than to wait until God's
grace is realized. God's grace is not simply a term in the Bible:
God's grace is an actual essence, a transcendental essence,
something that you cannot think, hear, taste, touch, or smell,
but something you can be aware of. Things of the spirit of
God can be known only through spiritual discernment. Not
through knowledge, not through the mind, but through spiritual discernment alone can you know that God's grace, the
transcendental presence, is here.

If the situation is to be met at all, it will be met that way. It
may be met by restoring harmony between husband and wife or
it may be met by bringing about a separation. There is no law
in any spiritual book that says two people have to stay together
forever. They may have come together for many human reasons
other than that God brought them together, but if God did not
join them together, their union can be put asunder.

Let no one believe that all marriages have been arranged in
heaven. Many marriages can be put asunder because God did

not form them to begin with. The activity of the presence of the Christ can unify where there is love or it can separate and divine where that is the way of demonstration. No practitioner or teacher can judge from the ultimate solution whether his work was successful or not.

### The Function of the Practitioner or Teacher
### Is To Bring a Realization of God's Grace to the Situation

Some years ago a business man who owned a half-interest in a business and wanted to sell it asked for my help. Many people came to buy and many deals came very near to being closed, but in the end, every one fell through. Nothing happened, and the sale was not made. Finally the man was convinced that my work was ineffective and asked me to stop. About a year later, he awakened one morning and asked himself, "Why should I sell my share of the business? Why don't I buy my partner out?" He did, and that became his most successful business venture. He is happier now than he has ever been, with a sense of completeness and fulfillment. He acknowledged, "I should not have asked you to sell my business but to bring God and His rightness into the situation, and now it has come."

No one can sit in judgment. Even if somebody is blind and says, "I would like to see. Will you restore my sight?" You can only respond, "I cannot work for a restoration of your sight. I can work only for the realization that God's grace be your sufficiency, and you will have to be satisfied with God's grace."

"Oh, no, no! I want my sight!"

"Well, then you will have to go to somebody else."

That is a very difficult position to be in. It is not easy to write letters to those asking for help for supply and say, "I am sorry, I do not know how. It is just something foreign to me. I can pray for you: I can realize God's grace for you; but I cannot ask God to give you something when I am already convinced that all that

God has, you already have, since you and the Father are one."

Some write and ask me to sell property for them and I reply, "Go to a real estate dealer. I am not a real estate dealer. I cannot sell property for you. I can realize God's grace, but that may not sell your property."

With a business problem it should be recognized that every activity of a legitimate business is a service. It is serving in one capacity or another, and every business that is conducted with the idea of integrity, service, and honesty becomes a Christ-activity. Any problem that is brought to practitioners, whether it is an unhappy household, a failing business, or the desire to establish a hospital or institution of some kind must be understood in the light of service unto the Christ, and then let the Christ perform Its function through the practitioner.

### The Teacher Must Have Attained the Consciousness of What He Teaches

The spiritual teacher cannot teach unless he has reached the state of consciousness that has realized the principles he is imparting, and then he can teach them only in the degree that he knows that he is educating the human mind out of itself, gradually getting the human mind to give up its reliance on its own powers of judgment, its reliance on good and evil, on money, and on princes and powers. Along with that comes the realization that there is no God-power to do anything to evil, so he cannot even seek a God-power. He can only abide in non-power. But the teacher cannot teach that unless he first knows it, and then, secondly, has in some measure attained.

The teacher will discover for himself that in the measure his human mind yields itself up is he attaining powers of discernment, the power to know the things of God, to tabernacle with God, to commune with God, but never for a purpose other

than the communion itself. Everything else is the Grace which
is added or comes forth.

### The Infinite Way Will Survive
### Only Because of Those Who Have Attained the Consciousness

If teachers have not demonstrated their inner contact
with the Father, there will be teachers looking for students,
looking for classes, and looking for fees. With such motiva-
tion no spiritual impartation is possible. If the message of the
Infinite Way is to function down through the ages, it will
function only through the consciousness of those who have
attained inner communion with the Father, the fruitage of
which is divine grace. Then it make no difference how few
there may be; those few will take care of the world because no
more of the world will be led to them than can be taken care
of by them.

The time has come for our teachers to present these specific principles and give the students the opportunity of working
inwardly with them until they attain some measure of oneness
with them. Then they can say, as did the Master, "I have overcome the world."[7] While Jesus had not overcome Caesar or the
Sanhedrin outwardly, he overcame both Caesar and the
Sanhedrin so far as his life was concerned. They could crucify
him, but they could not keep him in a tomb. They could shut
his mouth, but they could not stop his words.

Each one of you, in a measure, comes to where you have
overcome the world, meaning that the world comes to you as
temptation, but it finds nothing in you—no response. You can
walk up and down a great, long alley of whiskey bottles or gambling tables and not feel the slightest temptation. So, too, when
you have attained this consciousness, you can walk up and
down an alley of sin and disease, lack and limitation, or the
threat of war and fear no evil, because the temptation will be of

the same nature as those whiskey bottles or gambling tables. Eventually sin, disease, death, lack, and limitation will come to be recognized merely as pictures that find nothing in you to draw forth a response.

In that measure, then, those who seek the grace of God will, in coming to you, be released from this world, from the human mind, from its fears, temptations, and its two powers, so that you can rightly say that wherever the spiritually illumined walk, sin, disease, death, lack, and limitation evaporate. This may not happen insofar as the masses are concerned. All evil did not evaporate for everyone in the experience of the Master. Even he did not do many mighty works in his home or in Jerusalem. But evils do evaporate wherever there is anyone trying to break through the throng and seek enlightenment.

## ACROSS THE DESK

According to the human picture, a law of supply and demand operates in the distribution of goods necessary for human consumption and human needs. It is based on the assumption that a person needs something outside himself. So he looks outside and struggles to obtain the money with which to satisfy his needs. This whole process is a denial of the principle of Consciousness as the substance of all form.

Because Consciousness is omnipresent, there can be no such thing as a need, and man whose very nature is consciousness is not under the law of supply and demand. The infinity of his good is pouring through him. In this understanding, money appears in his experience as adequate, and always to be intelligently used, not for personal power or prestige, but for service.

Removed from under the law, man finds himself untouched by the apparent economic cycles, which then have no power either to give or take away. He lives free from the bondage to money or goods. His wealth lies in the spiritual riches of the kingdom "where neither moth nor rust," nor economic cycles, "doth corrupt."

TEACHING THE INFINITE WAY
"The Integrity Required of a Spiritual Teacher"

"Knowing God aright makes of a person the light of the world, and then the whole world, searching and seeking, is attracted to that light. The demands of the work force dedicated Infinite Way teachers and practitioners to work twice as many hours in the day and twice as many days in the week as almost anyone else, and unless they take their regular periods of meditation or, forgetting all the problems thrust upon them, just go and sit on the riverbank, they are going to become tense. Human effort will enter, both physical and mental, and if that happens, the message is lost.

"The teacher or the practitioner, to a far greater extent than any student, must divest himself of the little 'I.' He is not permitted to dwell much on what he would like, what he would like to do, what he would like to be, what he wants, or what he thinks he deserves. That 'I' has to disappear so completely that it is no longer a question of his desires or of his leisure. Now it is a question of fulfilling the demands that are made upon him, and he must have no other desire than to be the fulfillment of the activity given him to do. When that is all done, if he wants a little recreation—to look at television, go for an automobile ride, or take an inspirational book and just live with some of the great masters—that has its place, but not until he has fulfilled the function that he has drawn unto himself. He therefore has no right to complain about how much he has to do.

"The teacher and the practitioner are also in an unenviable position—not that a lot of foolish people do not envy them—because the teacher and the practitioner have to live up to what they are teaching. They cannot live so as to be a target for the condemnations of the students, and that calls for wisdom.

"A teacher should always remember that it is no disgrace not to know the answer to every question. No one can know everything. When students ask questions, if the teacher does not know the answer, he should be honest enough to say, 'I would rather get more information on this subject before I take it up,' or 'This is a subject that I do not care to discuss because I do not feel that it is a part of our work.' A teacher should never hesitate to admit that he does not know the answer. It is better not to answer than to mislead a student.

"When a question is on a specific facet of the Infinite Way, the teacher must be very careful not to answer it unless he is so thoroughly familiar with the writings on that subject that students cannot tell him later that he did not know what he was talking about. The teacher will maintain his dignity far more by postponing answering the question until the following week or the week after, and then speaking authoritatively, rather than just speaking out quickly for the sake of giving an answer.

"In teaching, whether it is with one student or a class, discussion is never permitted. If I have one patient or student in my office or if I have a whole class, my function is to reveal truth to them as it has been revealed to me. It is not my function to be concerned with whether they accept it or not; that is a point of receptivity within them. They come to me, and I give what has been given to me. The Infinite Way is really my personal religious life, my spiritual unfoldments and revelations, and I have set them down in books and on tapes and sent them forth. That ends my responsibility. I could not make anyone believe a single statement that he is not prepared to receive, and no amount of arguing, discussing, or debating would change anyone's mind about anything, not anything of a spiritual nature, at least.

"Our function is not to judge, to criticize, or to condemn, but to work toward that glorious day when all churches and all metaphysical movements will agree that there is only one God. If they are for God, they are for us; if they are not against us, they are for us."

Joel S.Goldsmith, *1963 Instructions for Teaching the Infinite Way.*

# Chapter Eleven

# Guidelines for
# Spiritual Unfoldment
# Through the Infinite Way

In most organizations there are rules which must be obeyed, even if at times better results might be accomplished in some other way. Since there cannot be one rule for one person and a different rule for another person, there has to be one rule which everyone must obey.

In the Infinite Way, although there is no organization in the sense of a set of rules, it is possible to have a minimum number of rules and at the same time be flexible so that there are occasions when the rules can be disobeyed. To illustrate this, I have suggested that tape group meetings should be opened and closed with a meditation, with no discussion before or after. That is a rule, and if the leader breaks it, it will mean that he has no interest in a successful tape group activity because it is impossible to discuss truth. Truth is a subject that does not lend itself to discussion because truth is not human; truth is not something that is dependent on your opinion or mine.

### *Truth Is God Revealing Itself*

In the class work there are times when a message comes

through that I knew nothing about until the moment it came through. It may have sounded strange to students who heard it, and they probably would have liked to discuss it with me. There was nothing to discuss, however, because I had nothing to do with the message coming through except to be a transparency for it.

There are many principles in the Infinite Way, but not one of them lends itself to discussion. I, myself, would not discuss them with anyone. I state them; the students take them or leave them, but I permit no discussion. This is because from the beginning of my work the principles that have come through have been proved practical and workable with me as well as with students. How then can I permit any argument about them?

At one time a publisher wanted to publish one of my books and after having it read by a member of his staff handed me a couple of pages of corrections. My answer was, "I welcome them. But first tell me how many healings the copy editor has been responsible for and how many years she has been practicing spiritual healing so that I will know that her corrections are better than my writing."

Either the principles of the Infinite Way are correct, and Truth has expressed Itself, or It has not. If the message is Truth expressing Itself, it will be known by its works. If not, it will go out of existence very quickly. The Infinite Way must stand, not on what I think of it or what students think of it, but on what it is. Therefore, I can prophesy—I won't forbid—but I can prophesy that those who permit discussions of this message will not be in the tape group activity for long.

Truth is an impartation that comes forth from the Spirit through the consciousness of an individual, and then it is received in the consciousness of the student as a seed. If the student keeps it locked up in his consciousness, thinks about it, ponders, and meditates on it, that seed will spring forth into fruitage. If it is not truth it will die stillborn. For this reason I have never permitted anyone to ask a question from the floor of any of my classes. Students may write questions and place them on the desk, and I will gladly answer them, but no questions are permitted from the floor. Then I am not breaking the rhythm of the impartation coming through me to the students, nor am I going to break into their receptivity just so that somebody may have the floor for his glory even for a moment.

### Conducting a Tape Group Activity

As I said before, a tape group meeting is opened with meditation, then the tape is played, followed by a closing meditation. Infinite Way work is in no sense a social activity. On the other hand, there is no reason why students cannot have breakfast, lunch, or dinner together because that makes for a harmonious relationship among them. That is something separate and apart from a lesson or a tape group meeting. Classes and tape meetings should be kept as free as possible from becoming discussion groups or coffee klatches.

At group meetings, in order to unify the group, it is a good idea to give the group either a quotation from the Bible or one from *The Infinite Way*[1]. In meditation a student should have one single point to dwell upon until it fades out and he becomes still and is listening. Such a quotation is helpful in centering attention on some specific principle.

For example, if a student meditated properly on "Man shall not live by bread alone, but by every word that proceedeth out of the mouth of God,"[2] it should bring the student to the place where he realizes that he does not have to worry about money, a position, or anything else in the outer world. What he has to have is a word from God. That breaks the attachment to the outer scene—the fear of it or even the reliance on it—because eventually everyone has to see that he does not live by money or by employment, but by the word of God.

So it is not the words a student reads in a book, but the Word, and that he must receive from God. A quotation is not God and is not going to supply anyone, but through its contemplation it will lead the student to where he actually knows that he must receive the word of God. If it takes thirty years, he might as well dedicate himself to that because only through receiving that Word can these other things be added unto him.

## Tape Recordings

Sometimes teachers are asked to recommend tape recordings of my classes for beginners. Actually, there will not be any beginners who ever come to the Infinite Way because anyone who has been led to this message is already something more than a beginner. It would be well to do away with the use of that word *beginner,* whether in reference to tapes, books, or classes. Let us not have any beginner's classes; let us not have any beginner's books or beginner's tapes. Instead let us have classes, tapes, and books of Infinite Way material that are basic.

Experience indicates that a very grave question arises that does more to prevent a student's progress than almost any other one thing. Everyone wants the most advanced teaching he can get, but very few are interested in building a foundation.

People who have never read an Infinite Way book or perhaps have read only one, write to me inquiring about the most advanced books and the most advanced tapes. Evidently they believe that they are capable of digesting and assimilating them. They are not. Such persons never will be anything but timewasters because it is as true in studying a mystical message as in studying mathematics or grammar, that without a foundation a person cannot achieve mastery of a subject. We have far too many dabblers in the arts and sciences, and in the spiritual life there are more than in any other field. Nobody seems to understand that foundational work is necessary. They ask and expect to be given illumination or initiation immediately because that is what they say they are seeking.

In recommending tape recordings, the teacher should always refer the student to those tapes that contain the foundational points of the Infinite Way on which mysticism and the healing consciousness are based. There is no way to develop the healing consciousness or Christ-consciousness without an understanding of the basic points.

The thing that has prevented many great spiritual leaders from attaining Christ-consciousness is that while they claim to know all about "I and my Father are one"[3] and all about the spirit of God, they are still accepting two powers and thinking of God in terms of God or Spirit over error. They are still thinking in terms of using God, or praying to God, and of expecting God to be their messenger. Until a student has really ruled out of his consciousness the idea that he can use God as his messenger boy to go out and do something for him, he cannot hope to develop the healing consciousness.

The basic and foundational tapes and books are essential for the development of spiritual consciousness. Among such tapes I can recommend the 1959 San Diego and Lausanne work, the 1960 Santa Barbara, Toronto, Grand Rapids, Holland, Lausanne, and Denver work, the 1961 San Diego and Lausanne work, and the 1962 Holland and Lausanne work.

All these contain basic foundational points and the application of these principles to daily human problems—not the use or the application of God, but the use and application of specific principles to the problems of everyday living.

## *Studying the Writings*

A tape group may be started by a student who may or may not have a healing consciousness. It often happens that when someone has a tape recorder he will invite his friends or students

to come to his home to hear the tapes. If the student conducting the tape group is a serious student, he will be hearing tapes,
reading the writings, probably attending classes, and his consciousness will be so filled with truth that sooner or later somebody in the group will ask, "Can't you give me help?" He will
find it embarrassing to reply, "I know all about the message, but
I can't prove or demonstrate it."

As a rule, however, as he continues with a tape group and
his study, a healing consciousness will develop. By this time
some of the group will inquire about the monthly letter, and he
will find it necessary to begin to teach the use of *The Letter*
which is an outline for study and practice. That is why I encourage every group leader to have one session a month to take *The
Letter* apart for the students, to show them how to pick out the
pearls, how to apply them, how to use them, and how to live
with them.

There are not too many persons in the world who are real
students and who can take the monthly letter and know how to
apply it to their daily living. They may read it and enjoy it. They
may have an uplift from it. They may even have a healing from
it, but they still do not grasp how to take the specific principles
set forth in each letter and work with them. In most cases it will
take someone who really understands the application of spiritual principles to teach members of the group how to study.

There should be some orderly procedure in teaching. Based
on my own experience, I recommend that students begin their
study with *Living the Infinite Way*,[4] spend a couple of days on
the "Introduction," and then go on into the book. Following
that, the student should devote two or three days to the
"Introduction" to *Practicing the Presence*[5] and then on into that
book. Why those two or three days on the "Introduction"?
Because it provides a foundation, explaining to the student the
object of the book, what he is to attain, why he is to attain it,
and giving him a reason for all that follows.

To read books of this nature without knowing why or what the expected result should be is folly. All that happens when a student merely reads a book without an understanding of its purpose is that he has read another book which was very sweet and pleasant to read, but nothing has been accomplished. After a few readings he should go back to the "Introduction" and ask himself, "Did I get out of the book what its purpose is?" If not, he must go back again, because these books are not just to be read: they are books that are to be worn out until new copies are needed.

Then I turn students to *The Art of Meditation* [6] and *The Art of Spiritual Healing,* [7] and from there on, into any of the books in any order. I always bring to light that the books of *The Infinite Way Letters,* however, are as important as any books we have, if not more so. Here in every chapter the student is introduced to certain principles and their application, so that he can always go to those books and find working tools. Also listed in *The Contemplative Life* [8] are specific chapters in the other books which are of paramount importance to the serious student because they contain the answers to almost every individual problem that can be brought to the student: family relations, specific illnesses, and supply. This is the way in which the books should be utilized.

I do not know when students will really understand what is in *The Thunder of Silence* [9] or in *A Parenthesis in Eternity.* [10] These two books are a hundred years ahead of the times, and the only way students will grow up to them will be to live with them.

No student is going to advance in the Infinite Way without an understanding of the foundational principles. On the other hand, no advanced student is going to succeed unless he keeps going back to the basic principles. It is my experience that occasionally I have to remind myself that I am not going to God to get a power. I have to remind myself once in a while that I am not seeking God to do anything to error. I do not know how anyone becomes so advanced that he can go beyond that. So I believe that when we recommend *Living the Infinite Way, Practicing the Presence, The Art of Meditation,* and *The Art of Spiritual Healing* we should do it from the standpoint that these are the books that contain the basic, foundational points on which the mysticism of the Infinite Way is built, and without which, the mysticism of the Infinite Way will never be understood.

In order to teach that mysticism, teachers will use *The Contemplative Life*, which might well be the first book to work with because it gently leads through contemplation into the deeper meditation. Then they should go on to *The Thunder of Silence*, which is divided into three parts, so that each part can be taught separately. The third and final part, "The Sermon on the Mount," should be a class entirely by itself, because these chapters really contain the height of mysticism.

From there the teacher could go to *A Parenthesis in Eternity,* and here, too, he would have to present the separate parts of this book, because it is graduated, going up in a very gentle upward slope. It is not wise to go into the subject of reincarnation, separate and apart from those chapters, because explaining that might be a personal opinion, but we are imparting it as a part of the mysticism of the Infinite Way.

In conducting classes, teachers could have classes on the fundamentals of the Infinite Way, and they could then have another series on living and applying the principles of the Infinite Way, and later, a third class on the mysticism of the Infinite Way.

### The Consciousness of the Individual Determines the Outer Activity

If the tape group leader has developed a healing consciousness, everything will unfold without instructions from anyone else. As the leader is called upon for help, gives it, and fruitage results, his practice develops. There is nothing more to it than providing the opportunity for the tapes to be heard, teaching the use of the monthly letter, practicing the principles, and doing the healing work, and that is about as far as a tape group leader can go.

And yet how impossible it is to make a rule like that because some tape group leaders have broken all the rules by becoming practitioners, teacher, and lecturers! Can you imagine my forbidding anyone who has a realized state of consciousness from engaging in any activity? So you can see that we can make rules only up to and including the playing of the tapes and the beginning of the healing work. After that each one evolves in accordance with his own unfoldment and attainment.

The one thing that I would like to make clear is that merely playing the tapes will not attract groups to anyone. Many students have started tape groups and found themselves with two, three, or four students and then one, or even as many as six, and then none, and finally they have given up.

Of course it would be very simple to say that there is something wrong with the tapes or with the city in which these students live, but that is not true. A person's demonstration is the activity of his state of consciousness, and an Infinite Way student must acknowledge this. No one can have a larger group than his consciousness can attract, nor will it ever be smaller than that, and it makes no difference in what city he lives. The city has nothing to do with it; the tapes have nothing to do with it; the books have nothing to do with it: it is the consciousness of the individual that is the all-important factor. Take the consciousness of the individual away from these books and these tapes and all that is left is paper and print and tape. Consciousness is what does the work.

There are Infinite Way practitioners in small and medium sized towns, and they have about as heavy a practice as they can take care of, and sometimes greater than they feel they want to take care of. On the other hand there are practitioners in large cities who may wonder if anybody in the town is sick at all.

The basic revelation of the Infinite Way is that the consciousness of the individual is the secret of life, and the degree of spiritual attainment determines the degree of the outer unfoldment. If a person has a healing consciousness, work will come to him, not only from his local community, but from all over the world. There is good reason for that. Since there is only one Consciousness, if a person has a healing consciousness, it will draw unto itself from the uttermost parts of the earth. If it is not a healing consciousness, those seeking healing will pass him by.

The entire aim of the Infinite Way is the development of one's own consciousness. That is why students have no right to want to save the world. They have no right to want to help their fellow man. Their only right is the development of their spiritual consciousness because when they have attained that they become the light, and those in darkness will find them and then they can be of help.

No one can be of help spiritually until he has the Spirit. Who would try to be a philanthropist before he had money? A person cannot give away what he does not have, and he cannot share the spirit of God until the spirit of God is upon him, but then he can begin to share It in the measure of his attainment.

All practitioners have gone through the experience of having a small practice in the beginning and sometimes a very small income, and sometimes none. That is not a new experience for beginning practitioners, but with study, meditation, and with a dedication to the development of consciousness, the practice grows, the student-body grows, and the income grows. All the outer experience conforms to the practitioner's state of consciousness.

So it is that those who start Infinite Way tape groups and do not have a healing consciousness should be willing to serve those who come, regardless of how few, but should at the same time be preparing themselves for the higher attainments so that eventually they can begin to teach the monthly letter and then later go as much further as their consciousness will carry them. Be assured of this, no one can stop you. Be assured that if I made any rule that would in any wise stop the progress of any one of our teachers, that teacher would go right on developing, if not inside the Infinite Way, then outside it, because no one can control consciousness. No one can make rules for consciousness. An individual will break out of any rule the moment his consciousness is prepared for it, but always remember, "by their fruits ye shall know them."[11] In other words, when students start evolving it must be as the fruitage of their developed consciousness.

### No Law Operates on the Person
### Who Has Attained the Consciousness of Grace

You, yourself, have discovered that you have had to work hard in your study and meditation and be faithful in attending classes and lectures to get to whatever state of consciousness you have attained. Nobody but you, yourself, knows what measure of dedication and devotion you have had to put into the message to arrive where you are. Do you believe that anyone is going to do it in any other way or in any easier way? You know better.

If teachers and practitioners have the real interest of the students at heart, the more they can make them realize the value of studying the message in all its forms, the better for them. Knowing the principles or being able to recite them will not demonstrate them for anyone. It is only when the realization of some specific principle or the realization of the Presence comes that students can say that no weapon that is formed against them can prosper.

Students must always be willing to place the responsibility where it belongs: on their state of consciousness. Their state of consciousness determines the outer picture, and if the outer picture is not yet harmonious or fulfilled, there is only one remedy: the further development of their consciousness and the attainment of a greater awareness of the indwelling Spirit. That is the point that many metaphysicians and those trained in metaphysics are apt to overlook. They are likely to believe that because they know statements of truth that that is it, and later they find that that is far from it. It is not knowing statements of truth: it is the attainment of the actual consciousness of truth that determines the nature of the outer demonstration.

Reciting "God with us," reciting "omnipresence," or reciting "omnipotence" does not make it so, nor bring the experience. There must be the God-experience, the actual experience of the Christ. There must be the dawning in consciousness of the spirit of God, the touch of God, the finger of God, the realization of God. It must be an experience before it can be lived. Otherwise students are living on the husks of words, statements, preachings, all of which are valueless.

In any Infinite Way work the measure of success is the healing ministry. I am speaking now of the work of teachers, practitioners, and tape group leaders. If someone comes to them to hear truth and they voice it and then he says, "Give me help." and the teacher or practitioner cannot give it, that is too bad. It should not happen.

Students should be willing to stay "in the city. . . until [they] be endued with power from on high."[12] Then they can go out in the spirit of the Lord, under the grace of God, because then they can say that there is no law. Moses gave us the law, but Christ Jesus did away with it. What need have students of law and what fear have they of law when they are under Grace! But they are not under Grace by reading books, hearing tapes, or going to classes. Books, tapes, and classes are the tools with which they work until they arrive at the consciousness of Grace. Once they have attained Grace, they are no longer under the law. There is no law of lack or limitation; there is no law to operate on them, in them or through them because they have risen above the law into Grace, not wholly, because no one has fully attained. But in proportion as the spirit of God is upon a person does he come more and more under Grace and this means less and less under law.

In proportion as the spirit of God is upon a person has he found his freedom, and it is not a freedom from anything: it is a freedom in Spirit, a freedom in and under Grace. The Infinite Way has no patent on it. It is true of everyone who has been touched by the spirit of God. It is not a phenomenon of the Infinite Way: it is a phenomenon of the spiritual universe and all who live under spiritual teachings.

Be guided by the Spirit. Some of you may ask, "How do I know when it is the Spirit?" My answer is by the fruitage. If you are having fruitage of a spiritual nature, of a constructive or positive nature, you are being guided. If the fruitage is not there, the answer is to study more, meditate more, and go deeper and deeper into Consciousness.

## ACROSS THE DESK

Thanksgiving is an opportunity to consider our abundant blessings and to give thanks to the source of them. Of all the reasons for thanksgiving, however, none is greater or more important for Infinite Way students than their gratitude for the work of Joel in giving us the Infinite Way.

While some spiritual teachers have left as a heritage a book or two or a few words written down by their disciples, we who follow the Infinite Way as our guide to illumination have been given some thirty books by the revelator himself and over one thousand hours of recordings of his class work exactly as it was given to his students, recordings in which Joel's consciousness has been captured. Thus students have ample material for spiritual unfoldment, and through the study of this material they will feel the impact of Joel's illumined consciousness which had attained the heights of awareness.

Although every student is free to read or hear whatever he

desires, to follow as many bypaths as he may choose, and to take as many lifetimes as he wants to attain the goal, those who are seriously working with Infinite Way principles will do well to work steadfastly with the writings of Joel and immerse themselves in his tape recordings until the goal of conscious union with God has been attained and they are living out from that high altitude of consciousness.

Those who approach that altitude of consciousness will be the laborers who "lift up [their] eyes, and look on the field. . . white already to harvest." The fruitage of that spiritual attainment is great, but greatest of all is that it assures that "peace which passeth all understanding" and this alone will mean for students the true thanksgiving.

This year let Thanksgiving Day be for us a very special time in which we set aside some time during the day an uninterrupted period to commune with the source of all good and release to the world the love that flows out from a grateful heart.

*Chapter Twelve*

# Christ-Consciousness As a Universal Experience

The first coming of the Christ is the coming of the Christ to individual consciousness, the Christ expressed as Moses, Elijah, Isaiah, Buddha, Lao-tzu, Jesus, John, Paul, and all who followed. With the evolution of consciousness, we are entering the period on earth which is referred to in scripture as the second coming of the Christ when that divine primal Consciousness will become the consciousness of all mankind, universally, and the new generation will not have to be taught metaphysics, mysticism, or religion, but will be born into it. That is about to take place.

Up to now religion has been on an individual scale and has been taught with the hope of bringing individuals to spirituality. Then the next generation comes into being, and the people have to be taught all over again because they were born into the same belief in two powers. By the time they were brought to some measure of understanding, they died, and the next generation was born, and again they had to be taught. That is going to be ended. Even the children of the next generation will be born into spiritual consciousness because now that this consciousness is being revealed on earth, everyone who comes to earth will come into Christ-consciousness.

### *Our Measure of Attained Spiritual Consciousness Becomes the Heritage of Future Generations*

Those of us on earth today and in times past were born into carnal consciousness because there was no other consciousness here. No matter of what religious persuasion we were, it was still a carnal consciousness, made up of good and evil, health and sickness, made up of the belief of a life-span of threescore years and ten, twenty, or thirty. In other words, we were born into a material state of consciousness, even if it was what might be considered a perfect material state. What we are now establishing is spiritual consciousness on earth. Through our reading, study, meditation, and practice, we have entered a measure of attained spiritual consciousness, and that is what is bearing fruit in our life.

Any measure of spiritual consciousness that we have attained is the measure of spiritual consciousness into which our students will come. Through them, we will discover how "ten"[1] righteous men can save a city. Ten individuals of attained spiritual light can provide a spiritual consciousness for a whole community. We are not engaged in merely healing sick persons or seeing that they are employed, enriched, or made happy. What we are doing is establishing the spiritual consciousness on earth into which the next generation can be born.

I wish that all the peoples of the earth could awaken to spiritual consciousness. But if we can realize how difficult it has been for us individually to awaken, even with the many helps we have been given, then we will have some idea of how difficult it is, if not impossible, for those who have not attained sufficient light to know that there is Light. It is highly probable that this present generation may depart from the earth not even aware of what has been taking place during their time here. The chances are that if a hundred years from now they could be told of what had happened while they were on earth, they might say, "How is it I never heard of it? I read newspapers and magazines every day and never knew such a thing was taking place."

Just as in 1776, there were a great many people who left this earth in their old Tory feudalistic consciousness, never knowing that an era of freedom and equality was being born. Only a remnant perceived the nature of what a world of freedom could be, a world which began with the vision given to Greece that produced the first freedoms there and which was next visible in England, resulting in the Magna Carta and the English law under which most of us in the United States live, which is a manifestation of the state of consciousness that was revealing freedom, justice, and equality.

Today we are manifestations of a state of spiritual consciousness now on earth, not building spiritual consciousness for students of the Infinite Way alone, but building that consciousness on earth as it is in heaven, that the coming generations may be born under Grace, not under the law. We will come and go, but our departure will take none of our attained spiritual consciousness with us. We are establishing spiritual consciousness on earth as it is in heaven for all the coming generations to be born into, to manifest, to live, and to express. The second coming of the Christ is what we are now establishing, Christ-consciousness as the consciousness of mankind. That is the work given us.

### *Evolving Consciousness Becomes the New Consciousness of Mankind*

The second coming of the Christ means that as Christ-consciousness is established within ourselves it is being established for the world, not necessarily for all the people who are now living in this world because they maybe too adamant to receive It and they will die. But the consciousness of the ten righteous men now evolving on earth will be the consciousness into which the new generations will be born.

The generations to come will not be born into an atmosphere of racial or religious bigotry and bias; they will not be born into a belief in two powers. I do not necessarily mean the children who are going to be born tomorrow or the day after tomorrow. I am merely stating my conviction that Christ-consciousness is now evolving on earth, and that as it continues to evolve the new generation will be born into that Consciousness. This second coming of the Christ means the universal coming of the Christ as the consciousness of mankind. In other words, future generations will be born into the consciousness we are now developing through study and meditation.

There are other ways in which we can see examples of that. The degree of education, culture, and refinement of our parents is what we were born into. There are different degrees of consciousness on earth, from the illiterate and the uncivilized up to the literate and the civilized, depending on the degree of developed consciousness into which a person was born.

When children are born into an age that has been given the revelation of God as individual consciousness, of one Power, of no condemnation, that is the consciousness into which the new generation will be born. It will be born into a consciousness of the true God and true prayer. It will not have to suffer through all the theological superstitions and ignorance of the past. Right now Christ-consciousness is evolving as the consciousness of mankind.

### The Breaking Up of the Old

In relationships between nations a great change is taking place. True, there are as many mistakes being made today in this awakening as there were in the days of the ignorance of spiritual principles, but at least the mistakes are not of the same nature, and therefore will not have the same destructive effect.

Nations are being given their freedom without having any capacity to maintain that freedom. Nations are being given the right to self-government that do not have the awareness of how to govern themselves, and therefore these nations will have to go through years and years of hardships. But this makes no difference, because during all these years of struggle they are gaining a knowledge of self-government, the education of the people is increasing, and they are headed in the right direction. The higher consciousness is breaking up the evil conditions that have existed on earth in order that better conditions may prevail.

Frequently we refer to "the good old days," but when some of the workers in factories are asked about what we call the good old days, they might deny that the days when men were receiving wages of a dollar a day were the good old days. The present-day evils really represent the breaking up of the evil conditions that were already in existence. In whatever direction we look, we will discover that nothing good is being destroyed: only the evils are being broken up by the activity of the Christ in consciousness.

During this transitional stage, some may suffer temporary losses, be thrown out of employment, and probably be forced to live on relief or a dole. Once the transitional period is over, however, through automation there will be a whole new world for everybody, for workers as well as for the users of products. Those who are employed will be employed at higher wages than the former ones were, and there will be a greater amount of products turned out for far less money. It is unfortunate for those who are the victims of these changes, but has that not always been the way of so-called progress?

People have gone to war to gain their freedom, have been wounded, maimed, and died, but later generations went on to live in freedom. Individual suffering in the human experience is inevitable while we are going through a transitional period of change. The only way to avoid it would be for everybody to become spiritual. But everybody does not have the capacity to turn to the Spirit or to benefit by spiritual wisdom, and therefore it is inevitable that some will suffer.

### *Benefits of the Activity of the Christ Will Be on an Individual Basis in This Generation*

The activity of the Christ is producing a new consciousness in which the old things will be wiped out and disappear, and a new world will be born. Some who have the capacity to stop praying for human betterment and to turn to the Spirit may even now receive the benefit of this higher consciousness. In fact, any Infinite Way student who finds himself with enough Grace to stop praying for improved humanhood and to turn within for a revelation of the kingdom of God and the peace that God gives can benefit whether he is twenty or ninety, as long as he can inwardly make the transition from praying to the God of spirit for earthly things. In any moment, in the twinkling of an eye, a person can be reborn, but only because divine Grace has led him to that place, and if he is receptive to this message he, at any age that he finds himself, can come into the new consciousness.

On the other hand, those who may be only twenty years of age, who have not yet been led to a spiritual message may go through the rest of their days without benefitting from the new consciousness. As the new generations are born, however, they are being born into the new consciousness, and there will be less warfare, bias, bigotry, prejudice, injustice, less of man's inhumanity to man, not because men are improving, but because some who are on earth are "dying" daily to their humanhood and being reborn of the Spirit.

Heretofore the attainment of Christ-consciousness has been

an individual experience. Now that attainment will be by birth; the new generation will be born into it. It cannot be a part of God's plan that one generation after another should be born into all the miseries that have existed on earth and that individuals in each generation emerge somewhat out of them, and then each succeeding generation would have to be born again to go through the same thing. No, God's plan is that the kingdom of God be universally established as the consciousness of every individual. God's plan is that the Christ, the son of God, be the only man.

### Human Consciousness Is the Prodigal Experience

Do you remember how the Prodigal Son left his Father's house, used up all his substance, and finally ended up eating with the swine? When he came to the realization that even his Father's servants were better off than he was, he started the return journey to the Father's house. The truth about this parable is that that was not the experience of a man.

The mystic who recounted this allegory was pointing out how the human mind left the divine consciousness, used up its substance and then turned back to the Father's house. The human mind is cut off from God; the human mind has no hidden manna, no meat that the world knows not of. The human mind is a prodigal. It has only what it knows it has, and each time it uses some of it, it has that much less. The Prodigal represents the universal human mind, and when it realizes that it has nothing left upon which to rely; it will be compelled to return to the Father's house.

This turnabout can never be done one by one, because the next generation would be born and would have to repeat the experience. So it can be done only as the human mind turns to spiritual resources. Only one generation has to come to the real-

ization that with all its material possessions and power, it is
nothing. It is less than a servant. But the servant of God is
always safe, always well, always fed, always housed, always
clothed, lacking nothing. The human mind, with all its store-
houses of wealth and power, is less than a servant, and the recognition of that makes it turn and brings about its reclothing with
the purple robe and the jeweled ring, so that individual consciousness becomes divine consciousness.

The parable of the Prodigal is not the experience of the
return of *a* man from mortality to spiritual consciousness, any
more than the experience of the Infinite Way is the attaining of
Christ-consciousness by individuals. The real meaning of this
parable is that the carnal mind of man must eventually surren-
der itself and ascend into Christ-consciousness.

What good is it to the world if one man centuries ago
became spiritual? Do you think that a mystic ever wasted a
moment telling about one individual who attained harmony?
Behind the parable of the Prodigal is the prodigal-consciousness
that today is eating with the swine, fearing the very prosperity
of the stock market, and fearing the abundance of the crops.

The consciousness of mankind today is the Prodigal Son
state, eating with the swine, enjoying the carnal pleasures of life
while threatened with every kind of danger: physical, moral,
and financial. This is the era of the return of the Prodigal Son
to the Father's house, of man's awakening from the world dream
of good in matter or in power, to the realization that even the
Father's servants are better off than he is, and of his march
toward the attainment of divine consciousness.

If the Prodigal alone could attain that, it would be of no
value to the world except as an example. If Moses could go from
being a shepherd to being the savior of the Hebrews, it would
be of value only as the experience of one person and the promise of what could be for us. If Christ Jesus could rise from the
consciousness of a Hebrew rabbi to the attainment of

Christhood, this would be of no value to us, except as an example and a promise of our possible attainment. If Saul of Tarsus could go from an unenlightened intellectual to the attainment of Christ-realization, its only benefit to us is as an example and a promise. But if the example and the promise are that only one by one can it be attained, there is no hope for mankind because each generation will have to go through the same experience, and only the remnant in each generation will ever attain it.

### The Coming of the Christ
### Universally to Human Awareness

The story of the Prodigal must be accepted as the rising of the carnal or human consciousness into the Divine, and this for mankind as a whole. The second coming of the Christ is not the second coming of one man with Christ-consciousness, but is the coming of Christ-consciousness to human awareness. Thereby not only a remnant will be saved: mankind itself will be saved and will have no more remembrance even of the smell of smoke. It is the state of divine consciousness that lives on earth without the awareness of any earthly problems, because it is Christ-consciousness manifest as mankind.

My life would be sad if I should ever have to believe that there is a divine grace which could bring to me the measure of harmony, joy, and peace that I have had in this world, and that it is not to be the gift of all coming generations, because then I would have given all these years in vain. My interest is not in building a little community of free souls. How could any community of free souls be happy knowing the rest of the world is in slavery?

The Infinite Way is demonstrating that the Prodigal's experience is the experience of man, man now aware that with all his power, crops, munitions, dollars, pounds, gold, silver, properties, he has nothing; he is bankrupt. In the knowledge of this, the consciousness of mankind starts on the journey back to the Father's house.

If through the teachings that have come through me, some measure of Christly freedom and peace can be attained for the world, then henceforth and forever the attaining of spiritual consciousness by any one person constitutes in a measure the attaining of spiritual consciousness by mankind, for God never imparts it to one person alone. The attaining of Christ-consciousness by any one of us is the endowment of that same spiritual consciousness on all who come within range of our consciousness, visible and invisible. It is the demonstration of the Christ on earth, Christ as the individual consciousness of mankind, the consciousness into which every child will be born. Every child will partake of this consciousness from the moment of birth; and not go through the long, slow, labored process of trying first to become good and then trying to become spiritual. Rather he will be born into spirituality.

### Educating Human Consciousness Out of Itself

As students have learned the specific principles of the Infinite Way, their spiritual consciousness has evolved and has become a healing, reforming, forgiving, and supplying consciousness for those who come to them, and has brought them to that place where they no longer live by outer effects of any nature, although they enjoy all of these that are necessary and desirable.

We do have meat the world knows not of; we do have a hidden manna; we do have a Grace which we have attained through this study, and now we can live by virtue of that divine grace without might and without power.

We are educating the human mind out of itself as we teach our students, and we are bringing them forth out of the power of the mind itself into an awareness that they have a meat the world knows not of; they have a hidden manna. They live by

Grace, by a sufficiency of Grace unto every moment. While we understand all this, let us be sure we have caught the broader vision. If we have thought that we have been teaching only those students sitting in front of us or with whom we are in correspondence, our vision has not been great enough.

We are teaching human consciousness; we are raising human consciousness and every time we have raised an individual we have raised thousands. The proof of this is that the principles which we have been teaching only to Infinite Way students and to those who have been led to us are now being accepted into religious, philosophical, psychiatric, and other activities of the world, showing that what we impart to students is really being imparted to human consciousness.

From the earliest years of his ministry, I have had the dream that it is possible to breathe the breath of life into mankind, that it is possible to impart to human consciousness these truths and states of consciousness which heretofore we have believed we were imparting to individuals. Throughout my ministry my goal has been attaining the day when every truth realized in my consciousness becomes the truth realized in the consciousness of mankind.

### How Can the Kingdom of God Be Established Universally?

The new message given to us is for the purpose of establishing the kingdom of God on earth as it is in heaven. How? Not merely by realizing that the studying that I am doing is benefitting my life, or the studying that you are doing is benefitting your life, but by recognizing that every truth realized in your consciousness or in mine becomes a law unto human consciousness.

That operates in the same way that every truth that becomes realized in my consciousness is becoming the law unto the lives of Infinite Way students, their minds, their bodies, their morals, and their supply. Every principle realized in our consciousness is becoming the law unto human consciousness. We may see it operate in some member of our family, in a neighbor, in a business, or in a political associate. But every realized spiritual truth in our consciousness is becoming a law unto this universe, and wherever we are, some measure of our divine consciousness is influencing those around us.

### Realized Spiritual Principles Form the New Consciousness

A truth realized in consciousness becomes a law unto consciousness. Can we confine it to one person? No, it does not become a law to a person: it becomes a law unto consciousness. Of course, the person most nearly attuned receives the first and greatest benefit, but eventually the circle widens. Even friends and relatives who cannot directly accept the message show forth some good. It is inevitable. A neighbor or a business associate may notice something in us and ask what we have. We may wonder why anyone knows that we have anything special because we have not told him. We do not have to. That is the beauty of it. It is shining in our faces. Then someone comes and asks, or even without asking, benefits.

We, who are realizing spiritual principles, are forming the consciousness of the new generation. All the spiritual wisdom of Lao-tzu, Gautama, Jesus, John, and Paul, all the spiritual wisdom of the mystics of the world has helped to form our consciousness. Without that, we would have been born savages. It was what was placed in consciousness by the mystics of the world that enabled us to be born as civilized human beings. A higher consciousness has evolved into this world, and we are all beneficiaries of it. So it is that every illumined consciousness has added illumination to the consciousness of the world.

Never before has it been known that every truth received in consciousness becomes a law unto consciousness. That has been revealed through the Infinite Way. Each truth that we consciously realize, we will realize as being established in human consciousness, and that will give greater power to the work that we are doing. Some of the earlier metaphysical work may have had as its purpose the improvement of the patient but now it is not only the patient that is improved: it is all human consciousness.

Before this truth was revealed and practiced, a very different attitude prevailed on earth. Oftentimes anyone who was not of our own household was hated, criticized, and malpracticed. But we are living in an era now in which consciousness is already so imbued with love that we are willing to forgive and to love our neighbor, whether our neighbor agrees or disagrees with us. Whether our neighbor is our friend or our enemy, we are willing to feed him, an evidence of the higher consciousness that has already come into being on earth. The second coming of Christ is here, and we are playing a part in Its unfoldment. One of the major ways in which we are doing this is by knowing that every truth realized in individual consciousness becomes a law.

### Going From Words and Thoughts to the Experience

The Infinite Way can bring about the complete spiritualization of consciousness, not because everybody in the world will become an Infinite Way student, but because every principle of the Infinite Way introduced into our consciousness is not being introduced into our consciousness alone, but into human consciousness. Every principle that has been released in Infinite Way writings is not being released merely into the consciousness of those who read the writings: it is being introduced into human consciousness.

Is it not the same idea as when news of a fearful nature makes even those people who have no knowledge of it begin to be fearful? Without knowing why, for no rhyme or reason, they waken in the morning with a sense of fear. They have unconsciously absorbed the universal hypnotism. Is there any reason, therefore, why the world cannot awaken one morning and realize its freedom? If we are communing secretly, silently, and sacredly within our own consciousness, are we not communing with the consciousness of everybody in the world who is trying to find a solution to these problems and wondering why God can't help? What difference does it make whether people are turning to a Buddhist God, a Hindu God, a Christian God, or a Hebrew God? Those are only mortal concepts. What the people are really turning to is the one God, and in proportion as truth enters consciousness the entire world is being evangelized.

Only the transcendental Presence Itself, the Christ, dissolves appearances. We must go beyond words and thoughts and recognize that there is no human thought that can help any situation. Our attitude must be, "Let me be still and know that *I* in the midst of me is God. Let me hear; let me receive." The listening period that follows may last ten, fifteen, or twenty seconds. The important thing is that we practice listening ten, twenty, or thirty times a day, whatever our own inner impulsion is.

There is never any lack of subjects upon which to meditate. Nearly always there is the threat of world war, of economic depression, of a flu epidemic, or of not electing the right candidates. There is enough going on in family, community, and national life so that a person could sit down a dozen times a day and ask, "How can this situation be met?" There is no human thought that will meet it. If truth-books could do it, there are more than enough of those published. If knowing the truth in the books could do it, there has been enough of that, too. The next step is the transcendental experience itself. For years the Infinite Way has been stating in every book that the Infinite Way is not a teaching: it is an experience. Whatever teaching there is, is merely to lead up to the experience.

We are in that era of the Infinite Way when every problem

must be approached from the standpoint, "There is no human thought I can think, nor is there any truth I can know with the mind that will solve this. Therefore, I must be about my Father's business. I must be listening, I must know that *I* in the midst of me is God, and let It utter Itself; let the voice utter Itself that the earth may melt. I am listening; I am developing a receptivity to truth."

Infinite Way practitioners very actively engaged in healing work are working from that standpoint. They have reached the understanding that human thought is not God's thought, and God's thought is not human thought. Human thought is not power. There is a higher consciousness, "the mind which was in Christ Jesus,"[2] and when It is on the scene, the earth of error melts. The effective meditation, prayer, or treatment is one in which the transcendental consciousness is realized and felt. When a practitioner can feel and know It, then It is on the field, and It is caring for the situation.

Teachers must take their more serious students into this higher consciousness—not teach them about it, but bring them to the actualization of it. The teacher's attitude should be, "I really should be able to turn out four, five, or six teachers and a dozen practitioners, but how? Not unless I can lift them to where they can realize that the activity of the human mind or knowing the truth with the human mind is not going to heal. If I am to be successful as a spiritual teacher, I must be able to lift students to that same realization of the transcendental presence to which I have access. Just as I feel that I have meat and hidden manna, so my function must be to bring students to where they can feel that same way and can go out into the world and do likewise."

In sending out the disciples Jesus must have raised them to some measure of his consciousness, certainly not enough, but to some measure of it, or they could not have gone out to do the healing and raising up which they did.

We cannot raise students to that level by simply teaching truth; we can do it only when they are willing to be lifted higher by these specific practices and made to realize that when we speak of the Christ we are not speaking about a term in the Bible: we are speaking about an actual Presence that is here and which is as tangible as their money in the bank is tangible to them. Until the Christ becomes that tangible to us as an experience, we do not have a hidden manna; we do not have meat the world knows not of: we have only quotations about it. Now we must come to the experience. The more there are with the experience, the sooner will the higher consciousness be the consciousness of all mankind.

If I have a healing consciousness, it will draw unto me my own, but if I find somebody in the same city with whom I am to share a practice, it does not lessen my practice: it is but multiplied. What happens is that some of the other person's patients and students come to me, and some of mine go to him, and it will keep on multiplying. So the more spiritually illumined students there are, the greater will be the activity.

### God's Grace Is Given to Us to Show Forth the Fruitage

The Infinite Way is not meant to glorify us or to make us healthy, wealthy, and wise. It is to show forth the Christ-consciousness, and the fruit of it is health, wealth, or happiness, but God did not intend it for you or me. How could anyone imagine such a thing as God revealing these truths of the Infinite Way to anyone for his benefit alone?

Let us never think for a minute that God's grace brought us to a message of this nature for our good. God's grace does not operate in that way. God's grace brought us to this message that we might show forth the fruitage of Christ-consciousness and thereby be instruments for establishing It on earth. Every truth we know; every healing that takes place through our consciousness is helping to establish that truth and that healing Grace in human consciousness. One of these days people will be talking this way as if this had always been the language. We will not be here, so we will not know that it has become a universal language unless, of course, in our rebirth some of us may be shown that we were here when all this was beginning, but otherwise we will come back to participate in it without ever knowing that we helped to initiate it.

### ACROSS THE DESK

The real significance of Christmas is lost when it becomes merely the celebration of an event that occurred nineteen centuries ago. With the advent of the realization of the Christ in consciousness, the meaning of Christmas deepens. The manger symbolizes the humility of self-surrender in our moments of meditation in which the tangible Christ-presence flows out through us to bless the world.

In these sacred moments the meaning of Christmas comes alive. We lay our earthly all at the feet of the realized Christ. We gladly give up all in order to commune with the Christ within. Christmas is thus renewed daily in our hearts and souls and released into the world in the healing power of the Christ-consciousness.

Joy to you this Christmas.

# About the Series

The 1971 through 1981 *Letters* will be published as a series of eleven fine-quality soft cover books. Each book published in the first edition will be offered by Acropolis Books and The Valor Foundation, and can be ordered from either source:

ACROPOLIS BOOKS, INC.
8601 Dunwoody Place
Suite 303
Atlanta, GA 30350-2509
(800) 773-9923
acropolisbooks@mindspring.com

THE VALOR FOUNDATION
1101 Hillcrest Drive
Hollywood, FL 33021
(954) 989-3000
info@valorfoundation.com

# Scriptural References and Notes

CHAPTER ONE

1. Romans 8:7.
2. Psalm 23:4.
3. John 8:58.
4. John 8:11.
5. Matthew 5:20.
6. II Corinthians 12:2.
7. Matthew 4:4.
8. John 8:32.
9. John 4:34.
10. Ezekiel 18:32.
11. John 10:10.
12. Luke 23:34.
8. Luke 17:21.
9. Romans 8:17.
10. Isaiah 45:2.
11. John 5:30.
12. John 10:30.
13. Psalm 46:6.
14. John 18:36.
15. Proverbs 3:6.
16. John 8:32.
17. Ezekiel 18:32.
18. Mark 12:31.
19. Matthew 25:45.
20. Matthew 25:36.
21. Proverbs 3:5.
22. Psalm 139:7.

CHAPTER TWO

1. John 14:6.
2. Exodus 3:14.
3. John 14:6.
4. Hebrews 13:5.
5. Matthew 28:20.
6. John 6:20.
7. Luke 24:49.

CHAPTER THREE

1. John 9:25.
2. I Kings 19:12.
3. I Samuel 3:9.
4. Acts 10:34.
5. John 8:32.
6. John 18:36.
7. Hebrews 4:12.

CHAPTER FOUR

1. John 18:36.
2. Job 27:7.
3. Galatians 2:20.
4. Exodus 20:5.
5. Matthew 3:15.
6. John 10:10.
7. Romans 8:11.
8. John 6:45.
9. Matthew 28:30.
10. By the author
    (Acropolis Books,
    Atlanta, GA., 1996).

CHAPTER FIVE

1. Habakkuk 1:13.
2. John 18:36.
3. Matthew 5:39.
4. Matthew 26:52.
5. John 9:25.
6. Joel S. Goldsmith.
   "Across the Desk" in the
   Chapter "Contemplative
   Meditation," *The
   Contemplative Life*
   (Acropolis Books,
   Atlanta, GA., 1999).
7. *Ibid.,* pp. 108-109.
8. Matthew 13:46.
9. Psalm 23:4.
10. Genesis 18:32.
11. The work given in the
    1959 Classes is
    embodied in Joel S.
    Goldsmith's *Realization
    of Oneness.*
12. Isaiah 45:2.
    Teaching the
    Infinite Way
13. Isaiah 2:22.

CHAPTER SIX

1. By the author.
   (DeVorss Publications,
   Camarillo, CA).
2. Acts 17:28.
3. Habakkuk 1:13.
4. Revelation 21:27.
5. Matthew 12:45.
6. I Kings 19:12.
7. Matthew 4:4.
8. John 5:30.
9. Matthew 25:40.
10. Matthew 6:10.
11. Acts 3:6.
12. John 12:45.
13. Psalm 24:1.
14. Luke 15:31.

CHAPTER SEVEN

1. John 18:36.
2. Matthew 4:4.
3. Luke 12:22,31.
4. Philippians 2:5.
5. John 10:10.
6. I John 1:5.
7. Psalm 16:11.
8. Galatians 6:7,8.
9. I Corinthians 2:14.
10. Romans 8:10.
11. Luke 15:31.
12. Matthew 13:46.
13. Matthew 17:5.

CHAPTER EIGHT

1. Psalm 23:4.
2. By the author (out of print).
3. By the author (Acropolis Books, Atlanta GA. 1998).
4. By the author *Realization of Oneness.* (Acropolis Books, Atlanta, GA.).
5. Matthew 6:33.
6. Matthew 10:19.
7. Psalm 46:10.
8. Galatians 2:20.
9. Matthew 18:22.
10. Matthew 4:4.

CHAPTER NINE

1. John 10:30.
2. John 13:36.
3. John 9:25.
4. Matthew 5:39.
5. Matthew 26:52.
6. By the author (Acropolis Books, Atlanta, GA., 1996).

CHAPTER TEN

1. Luke 12:14.
2. John 8:11.
3. Philippians 3:12.
4. Leviticus 19:18.
5. Matthew 25:40.
6. John 9:25.
7. John 16:32.

CHAPTER ELEVEN

1. By the author (DeVorss
   Publications, Camarillo,
   CA., 1998).
2. Matthew 4:4.
3. John 10:30.
4. By the author. (Harper
   Collins, New York,
   1993).
5. By the author.
   (Acropolis Books,
   Atlanta, GA., 1997).
6. By the author. (Harper
   Collins, New York,
   1990).
7. By the author.
   (Acropolis Books,
   Atlanta, GA., 1997).
8. By the author.
   (Acropolis Books,
   Atlanta, GA., 1997).
9. By the author. (Harper
   Collins, New York,
   1993).
10. By the author. (Harper
    Collins, New York,
    1986).
11. Matthew 7:20.
12. Luke 24:49.

CHAPTER Twelve

1. Genesis 18:32.
2. Philippians 2:5.

# Joel Goldsmith
# Tape Recorded Classes
# Corresponding to the
# Chapters of this Volume

~

Tape recordings may be ordered from

THE INFINITE WAY
PO Box 2089, Peoria AZ 85380-2089
Telephone 800-922-3195 Fax 623-412-8766

E-mail: infiniteway@earthlink.net
www.joelgoldsmith.com
Free Catalog Upon Request

Chapter 1:   THE NEED FOR RELIGION
             #550   *1963 Instructions for Teaching the
                    Infinite Way* 6:2

Chapter 2:   GOD AND PRAYER
             #508   *1963 Instructions for Teaching the
                    Infinite Way:* 4:1

Chapter 3:   "NOW I SEE"
             #509   *1963 Instructions for Teaching the
                    Infinite Way:* 1:1

Chapter 4: THE PARENTHESIS
#510 *1963 Instructions for Teaching the*
#511 *Infinite Way* 2:2 and 3:2

Chapter 5: INFINITE WAY PEARLS
#509 *1963 Instructions for Teaching the*
#511 *Infinite Way* 1:2, and 3:1

Chapter 6: NOT APPEARANCES BUT *IS*
#510 *1963 Instructions for Teaching the*
*Infinite Way,* 2:1
#90 *the 1954 New York Practitioners' Class* 2:1

Chapter 7: MATERIAL SENSE OF DEMONSTRATION OR THE
UNFOLDMENT OF GRACE
#550 *1963 Instructions for Teaching the*
*Infinite Way,* 6:1

Chapter 8: INFINITE WAY PROTECTIVE WORK
#550 *1963 Instructions for Teaching the*
*Infinite Way:* 6:2

Chapter 9: THE SIMPLICITY OF THE HEALING TRUTH
#551 *1963 Instructions for Teaching the*
*Infinite Way* 7:1

Chapter 10: EDUCATING THE HUMAN MIND OUT OF ITSELF
#520 *1963 Kailua Private Class,* 5:1&2